IMAGES
of America

KILLINGLY REVISITED

NEW TOWN CLOCK. The Danielson Main Street Incoporated organization received partial funding by a grant from the Quinebaug Shetucket Heritage Corridor to replace the original late-19th-century timepiece that once stood downtown. The new clock was placed in a flower bed and topped with a sign denoting the town's incorporation date to enhance the historic district of Danielson. The dedication ceremony was held on December 6, 2006.

On the cover: Mary Salotti (center) became owner of the New York Fruit Company and Candy Store in Danielson in 1913. She had been proprietress of another such store in Danielsonville since 1886. The store was well stocked with choice confectionery, fruits, nuts, soda, ice cream, cigars, and tobacco. A partnership of Louis Bertorelli and Joseph Cristina took over in 1924. In 1928, Bertorelli became sole owner. (Courtesy of Patricia Bertorelli Belade.)

IMAGES
of America

KILLINGLY REVISITED

Natalie L. Coolidge

ARCADIA
PUBLISHING

Copyright © 2007 by Natalie L. Coolidge
ISBN 978-1-5316-3148-2

Published by Arcadia Publishing
Charleston SC, Chicago IL, Portsmouth NH, San Francisco CA

Library of Congress Catalog Card Number: 2007927695

For all general information contact Arcadia Publishing at:
Telephone 843-853-2070
Fax 843-853-0044
E-mail sales@arcadiapublishing.com
For customer service and orders:
Toll-Free 1-888-313-2665

Visit us on the Internet at www.arcadiapublishing.com

This book is dedicated to all who live, have lived, or hope to live in the town of Killingly. Join us on a 300 year memory trip and then consider how you can help preserve the memories of the next 100 years.

Respice, adspice, prospice
"Look to the past, the present, the future"

CONTENTS

ACKNOWLEDGMENTS

The members of the Killingly Historical and Genealogical Society were excited when the timely telephone call came from Dawn Robertson at Arcadia Publishing inviting us to produce a follow-up to our first book in the Images of America series, *Killingly*. We had been searching for just the right project to undertake in celebration of the town of Killingly's tercentennial and here was the solution to our dilemma.

The majority of photographs in this new book, *Killingly Revisited*, are from the society's files. Many were donated after our first book was published. Our thanks go to Richard Ouellette, Gilbert Poirier, Patricia (Bertorelli) Belade, and Joseph Chauvin, who cared enough to take or save photographs for the enjoyment of the generations who will follow us. I personally give an extra special thank-you to Marilyn Labbe for her tireless research that has provided new information for the captions, to Lynn LaBerge for her able leadership of the society as its president and custodian of the photograph collection, to Charles Rhodes for his photography skills, and to Louis Leveillee at the Killingly Public Library for all his help. We are indebted to historians of the past and present who committed their observations to the printed page so that we might increase our knowledge of our hometown as it celebrates its 300th birthday. Information was gleaned from Ellen Larned's *History of Windham County, Connecticut*; Allen B. Lincoln's *Windham County, Connecticut*; *Miles of Millstreams* by Margaret Weaver and Geraldine and Raymond Wood; *Mills Along The Whetstone Brook* by Richard C. Adams; *The Making of Danielson* by H. V. Arnold; *History of Education, Town of Killingly, 1650–1976*, produced by the members of the Heritage Sub-Committee of the Killingly Bicentennial Commission; *Historic Resource Survey of Killingly, Conn.*; *Gazetteer of the States of Connecticut and Rhode Island* by John C. Pease and John M. Niles; the Killingly Economic Development Office; and the *Windham County Transcript* and *Norwich Bulletin*.

I am especially thankful for the moral support of my 93-year-old mother, Ruth LaFantasie, and for her memories of the town that was her home for most of her life.

INTRODUCTION

The town of Killingly has entered the 21st century and will be celebrating its tercentennial during the year 2008. It is a good time to reflect on the history of the town and its people.

It is interesting to study the geological heritage of northeastern Connecticut and discover how different it is from the rest of the United States. It began its formation more that 500 million years ago as the Earth's tectonic plates moved back and forth, eventually creating Pangaea (a prehistoric giant super continent) that then split apart to form the continents as we know them today. Here in Killingly, we sit atop the remnants of the ancient Iapetus Ocean and a former chain of islands known as Avalonia. Our area's makeup is different than that of the rest of the United States because of this. There is a definite line of demarcation between the two on a bedrock map of Connecticut by John Rodgers that is called the "Lake Char Fault" for the Native American name of Webster Lake in Massachusetts. It bisects Killingly and runs close to the intersection of Route 12 and Attawaugan Crossing Road according to Killingly's town historian, Margaret M. Weaver.

Our hills are the result of a collision of several plates that formed the Appalachian Mountains that were once the world's largest. Our landscape has been shaped and reshaped due to our geologic history of tectonics, glacial activity, earthquakes, and volcanism. The Ice Age and the melting of the glaciers contributed to the factors that eventually made Killingly into the industrialized place it is today. The millions of rocks that farmers have had to clear from their fields and have been used to make the picturesque stonewalls of New England were dropped here by those glaciers. The sand and gravel banks, as well as the deposits of clay that were used for brick making, were not located here just by chance but by grinding ice and water run-off. The silt deposits from the Five Mile River created the "land between the rivers" on which James Danielson first settled. The brooks and rivers caused the erosion and shaping of riverbeds and falls. All these factors came together to make Killingly a desirable site for manufacturing and thus a good place for people to call home. (This is a short, simplified description of the fascinating story of "how it all began.")

Long before the white man arrived to settle the land, a band of Native Americans lived near the great falls of the Quinebaug River at the conjunction of the Quinebaug and Five Mile Rivers. Corn was their chief crop, but they also raised beans, Native American turnips, squash, pumpkins, artichokes, and tobacco. They had constructed a fort on a low hill just below the falls. Many flint arrowheads have been found in that area. The town abounds in Native American place names that have continued in use through the years. One of the items sought after by the Native Americans from great distances were whetstones or scythe stones used for sharpening knives. The Native Americans got them from a quarry near the mouth of the Mahmunsqueag meaning "the spot resorted to for whetstones" (Whetstone Brook) in the Elmville section of Killingly, before it flows into the Assawaga (Five Mile) River. Because of its importance, the range of land northward and southward was known to them as the Whetstone Country.

The township of Killingly, as it was laid out in 1708, was described as "the wild border land between the Quinebaug and Rhode Island" by historian Ellen Larned. "Rough hill ranges, alternating with marshes and sand-flats, offered poor inducements to purchasers and settlers." There were few public roads through the land, and it might not have been settled at that time except for one big advantage: the Colony of Connecticut owned it instead of individuals or corporations. The land, therefore, was deemed good enough to be granted to pay creditors or reward men for civil and military services. Under those grants, the first men to take possession of land in the Whetstone Country were Maj. James Fitch and Capt. John Chandler.

Major Fitch received his grant of 1,500 acres by the General Court in 1690, and he immediately laid claim to the most desirable part of the whole tract that lay along the Quinebaug and Assawaga Rivers. Captain Chandler's grant was high land two miles east of the Quinebaug River that later was called Killingly Hill on what is now Putnam Heights.

Richard Evans was the first white settler in 1693 on a 200-acre claim laid out near the junction of the present Route 44 and Route 21 in Putnam. It was in the northern part of what became Killingly but which is now included in Putnam. Several other tracts of land were claimed but no other settlers followed Evans because of Native American troubles.

In 1707, James Danielson purchased the triangle of land between the Quinebaug and Five Mile Rivers from Major Fitch, making him probably the earliest settler within the borough of Danielson. The general assembly was petitioned by 30 families residing east of the Quinebaug and north of Plainfield and were granted the privilege of forming and incorporating a town in 1708. Gov. Gurdon Saltonstall named the new town Killingly. Its boundaries ran from Rhode Island on the east to the Quinebaug River on the west, and from Massachusetts on the north to Plainfield on the south. The remaining unclaimed lands within the town were granted to 44 proprietors the next year.

The early settlement of the town was in the northern section, especially around Killingly Hill that is now along Route 21 on Putnam Heights. There the people built their church, small shops, and taverns in the mid-18th century. The town records for the first 20 years were misplaced or destroyed. Later, in 1855, that section became part of the town of Putnam.

A group of Massachusetts settlers purchased 2,400 acres in 1711 from John Chandler in the area now called East Killingly. The Chestnut Hill Purchase was the first permanent settlement within the present boundaries of Killingly. The last region to be settled was South Killingly; this was done in 1721, when Jacob Spaulding of Plainfield built the first home there. After this period of settlement, the people of the town got down to the business of building roads, bridges, and schools and taking care of the poor.

The 1800s saw the beginnings of the factories that soon flourished along the waterways of the town. Woolen mills and cotton mills as well as sawmills, grain mills, and tanneries dotted the landscape. There was even a gin distillery and a paper hanging manufactory. In 1810, the population was 2,542, and there were about 350 dwelling houses and three companies of militia. There were 21 school districts and primary schools, four social libraries, six mercantile stores, two post offices, five clergymen, six physicians, and one attorney. Men, women, and children were employed and worked extremely long hours at low salaries. Men were paid $5.22 per week; women, $2.20 per week; and children under 20, $1.50 per week, until laws were passed to ensure that children received proper schooling.

The opening of the railroad in 1840 changed many things in the town of Killingly. Dayville Depot became a shipping center for Killingly Center, Williamsville, Chestnut Hill, Ballouville, and Attawaugan. The location of the new depot in West Killingly necessitated the building of a new street (present-day Main Street) and opened up the development of a new commercial district that then became Danielsonville in 1854.

The early name of Danielson was Danielsonville, and Dayville was called Daysville. It was not until 1895 that the citizens voted to drop the "ville" and shorten the name to Danielson. In 1899, they voted that East Brooklyn was no longer part of the borough of Danielson.

During the 1900s, our townspeople served their country in times of war, suffered in times of depression, and enjoyed times of prosperity. The Danielson Industrial Foundation was formed to attract industries that were not related to the textile industry, which was moving south and creating much unemployment. Their success brought many new businesses into the old factories or new ones were built. The town now has an Economic Development Commission to carry on the Danielson Industrial Foundation's work, and it continues to vigorously market the town of Killingly.

The completion of the Connecticut Turnpike in 1958 was of significant importance to the growth and prosperity of the town. An airport was dedicated July 4, 1962, off Maple Street in Danielson. The Dayville area around the junction of Routes 101 and 12 and Interstate 395 has seen tremendous commercial and industrial development from 1980 to the present.

Statistics show that the town of Killingly covers 50 square miles and as of 2006 had a population of 17,675. Economically, as of 2005, manufacturing still employed the largest number of the population (35.9 percent), with trade (27 percent) and services (21.6 percent) close behind. The top five major employers are Frito-Lay, Brooks Maxi Drug Warehouse, the Town of Killingly (including the Killingly Board of Education), Staples Distribution, and United Natural Foods.

People living in the 20th century have seen so many great changes in the way they live, work, and play that it is hard to keep track of them. Modes of transportation moved from horses, to trains, to automobiles, to airplanes, and now to space travel. Shopping centers and malls changed the shopping habits of the townspeople. Stores within the business districts of the villages experienced a decrease in shoppers and had to become more creative in their promotions. Shops changed from the type where clerks took all items off the shelves for the customer to the modern self-service stores. Gasoline service stations changed from full service to requiring drivers to pump their own gas. Housewives changed from using wood stoves to gas or electric ranges, microwaves, and convection ovens. Telephone technology has changed, and they have become smaller and smaller with added features that our ancestors never would have dreamed of. Simple forms of recreation and entertainment became more technical with the invention of radios, movies, television, phonographs, videos, CD players, and DVDs. Imagine taking a photograph or video with your telephone. Computers are responsible for completely changing our way of life. They have evolved from gigantic machines requiring large buildings to house them to small, hand-held instruments.

We can only imagine what the 21st century has in store for us!

WELCOME SIGN, DANIELSON. Welcome signs were erected in four locations in November 2006 on behalf of the Economic Development Commission and Danielson Main Street Incorporated. These attractive signs welcome visitors and citizens to the town of Killingly and direct them to the Downtown Historic District. Danielson's Main Street is a National Historic Main Street District, and the signs tout the historic buildings that house a variety of shopping opportunities.

One

MILLS

Killingly owes its early prosperity to the establishment and growth of mills built along its waterways. First came the sawmills and gristmills providing life's basic materials—the lumber to build homes and the grain to feed families. By 1789, William Cundall had established a woolen mill in the vicinity of Danielson.

After Eli Whitney's invention of the cotton gin in 1793, it became practical to manufacture cotton fabric in a factory environment. Soon attractive sites along brooks and rivers in the area were utilized and dams were built. Killingly's factories were so successful that historian John Warner Barber reported the town as, "the greatest cotton manufacturing town in the state" in 1836.

The Whetstone Brook, which originates in East Killingly and drops almost 200 feet before it joins the Five Mile River in the Elmville section of Dayville, was home to many mills along its banks. One of its falls is capable of generating an estimated 400 horsepower. Equally as important is the Quinebaug River and the point in Danielson where it meets the Five Mile River.

In the 1930s, Killingly was known as "Curtaintown, USA" because of the production of curtains and materials by the factories of Powdrell and Alexander. As the textile mills later pulled out of New England to move to the South, the town looked for diversified industries. One of the first to arrive in 1913 was the Goodyear Tire and Rubber Company of Akron. In 1940, V. LaRosa and Sons of New York City built a modern plant to make macaroni products. The Dayville Development Corporation was a special corporation formed by the Danielson Industrial Foundation to raise money to bring Knox Glass to the community. The plant for making glass bottles was built and opened in 1958. The latter half of the 20th century saw the creation of an industrial park with such nationally known corporations as Frito Lay, Staples, and United Natural Foods.

As the 21st century unfolds, the Killingly Economic Development Commission continues to promote the advantages of locating businesses within the borders of the town of Killingly.

WHETSTONE BROOK. The Whetstone Brook originates from the spring-fed Old Killingly Pond in East Killingly. From here, it travels through an extensive reservoir system built by the Chestnut Hill Reservoir Company between the years of 1828 and 1872. When filled to capacity, these reservoirs could hold nearly a billion gallons of water. After leaving the reservoir system, it makes a rapid descent of more than 70 feet in its first 200 yards. In the photograph above, the Whetstone Brook rushes by the Judge Young Mill in East Killingly. Below are the falls at Cat Hollow in the Elmville section of Killingly.

QUINEBAUG AND FIVE-MILE RIVERS. Killingly's reputation as "the greatest cotton manufacturing town in the state" came as a result of the location of its mills on the Quinebaug and Five Mile Rivers, as well as their tributaries. Enterprising businessmen were eager to invest their capital in water privileges with large volumes of water. The Five Mile River in North Killingly was the site of the early Talbot gristmill and later Howe's Factory. The photograph above shows the great falls of the Quinebaug. The one below shows the confluence of the two rivers just below the falls in Danielson as they continue to make their way south. (Above, courtesy of Joseph Chauvin.)

OLD TIFFANY MILL. About 1827, Comfort Tiffany erected a small wooden cotton mill about 100 yards below the falls at the mouth of the Five Mile River. It had 1,000 spindles and 24 looms, employed 34 hands, and consumed 40,000 pounds of cotton to make 150,000 yards of 7-8 shirting material. The mill was deeded to the Quinebaug Company on January 7, 1848. (Courtesy of the Gertrude Pradel Collection, Killingly Historical and Genealogical Society.)

FALL BROOK MILL. George A. Niles ran the Fall Brook Mill from about 1860 to 1876. T. F. Bailey was the proprietor in 1888. Niles specialized in the sale of fresh ground Nova Scotia Plaster used as a garden fertilizer. A gristmill and sawmill were also located one mile south of Danielsonville on Green Hollow Road providing farmers with corn, cracked corn, and meal for sale. (Courtesy of the Gertrude Pradel Collection, Killingly Historical and Genealogical Society.)

HULET SAWMILL. It is believed that the sawmill was built by Jacob Hulet and later operated by his son, Joel, in the Mashentuck section of Killingly. The mill ran one of the old-fashioned, up-and-down saws, in a building about 20 by 40 feet, and boards, shingles, and so forth suitable for the domestic needs of the time. The Smith-Mann House on the northwest corner of Mashentuck and Cook Hill Roads was built by Jacob Hulet around 1800 and later sold to his son, Joel, in 1838. Mashentuck Mountain is in the left background. From the earliest times of settlement, there was a great need for sawmills and gristmills to be located near streams to provide their power. Richard Bartlett built his in the narrow gorge at the head of the rapids on the Whetstone Brook. At the Peeptoad Mill site, squire Tom Durfee owned an axe and hoe shop. Nicholas Cady owned a sawmill and gristmill on the Whetstone Brook about 1715. It may have been close to what is now Elmville. Another was located on the Five Mile River in Danielsonville.

STONE HOUSE AT DANIELS VILLAGE, AROUND 1850. Visible to the left of the stone house are several of the frame houses that were part of the mill village but are no longer existent in the northern section of Killingly near Stone Road in Pineville. The site is listed in the National Register of Historic Places as the location of one of the first textile mills in Connecticut. (Courtesy of Richard Ouellette.)

SAYLES AND POTTER WOOLEN MILL, 1866. Phebe Sayles and Sarah Potter owned the Killingly Center mill on Cat Hollow Road in 1866. Sometime before 1889, Timothy E. Hopkins purchased it to produce fancy cashmeres. By 1915, it was known as the Killingly Worsted Company and was run by William K. Litch. It was sold to Morris Fisher in 1953 and leased by Hale Manufacturing Company in 1954 for the next 20 years but burned in 1978. (Courtesy of the McEwen Collection, Killingly Historical and Genealogical Society.)

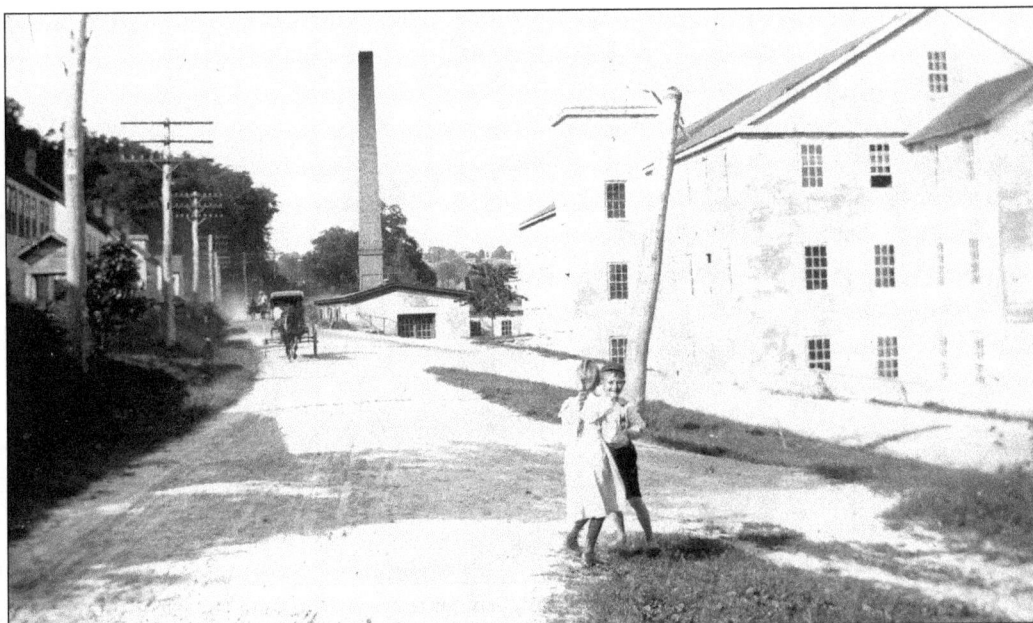

DAVIS AND BROWN, VALLEY ROAD, EAST KILLINGLY. Children play in the road in front of one of the oldest mills on the Whetstone Brook. The mill utilized the waterpower to manufacture cheviot and Tibet cloths of medium grade but also had an auxiliary steam plant. They employed about 70 hands. A general slump in the woolen manufacturing business in 1914 caused the mill to close. Davis and Brown was purchased from Chase Mill in 1916 and continued until the mid-1930s. In 1940, N. Lorne Greig of Dayville purchased the plant and operated as Greig Mills, Incorporated. In 1954, he sold the business to Hale Manufacturing Company. The photograph below shows the new smoke stack being constructed at Davis and Brown. (Courtesy of Henry Hopkins.)

WHETSTONE CONDOMINIUMS. The end of the 20th century saw the old Davis and Brown mill converted to a new use. Condominiums were created from the old factory building at 501 Valley Road, East Killingly.

WILLIAMSVILLE MANUFACTURING COMPANY. In 1826, Caleb Williams of Providence bought 27 acres, along with the privilege to use waterpower from the Quinebaug River, from Asa and William Alexander and John Day. Williams built a factory village, which he named Williamsville. In the late 1820s, Williamsville consisted of little more than the tenant houses and the mill, which was equipped to make cloth from bales of cotton. (Courtesy of the McEwen Collection, Killingly Historical and Genealogical Society.)

18

QUINEBAUG COMPANY, EAST BROOKLYN. The Quinebaug Company was incorporated in 1851, however, the mill was built several years earlier. Comfort Tiffany had built a small wooden cotton mill on the riverbank about 1827, later transferring the mill property, waterpower, store, and tenements to the Quinebaug Company. Note the round building used to store gas for lighting purposes. In 1873, about 600 hands produced 600,000 yards of sheeting and shirting each month. The mill was destroyed by a terrible fire in April 1961. In the photograph below, the men were employed in the Quinebaug Company. The man with the vest and necktie was the second overseer in the cloth room. Mr. Nash was the foreman in the lower photograph. (Above, courtesy of the McEwen Collection; below, courtesy of Henry Hopkins.)

UNCAS KNITTING COMPANY, 1883. Emanuel and Christopher Pilling built a hosiery factory, a new industry for the town, on School Street in Danielsonville. It was known first as the Assawaga Mill and later as the Aspinock Knitting Company. One of its products carried the trademark Waukenhose, made to conform to the shape of the human foot. The wooden building burned and was replaced by a brick mill. (Courtesy of Richard Ouellette.)

ABNER YOUNG HOUSE. Abner Young's home was on the west side of Main Street, second from the corner of Academy Street in Danielson. Young ran a shoe factory on Mechanic Street for 17 years and employed over 400. He also was a carpenter and president of the First National Bank of Killingly. The house was demolished April 20, 1960, to make way for the office of Southern New England Telephone Company.

20

DAYVILLE WOOLEN COMPANY. The Dayville Woolen Company was organized on March 17, 1894, on Main Street in Dayville and began operating in the former Sayles Company mill. In 1903, the successor of the Dayville Woolen Company was incorporated under the name of Assawaga Company. In later years, it was purchased by wire manufacturer William Prym and Company. (Courtesy of Thomas Guillemette.)

WOMEN AT WORK, 1850. In the 1850s, employees worked 69 hours a week. The factories operated by lamplight, fueled by fish oil, during the fall and winter months. On Saturdays, the workday ended at 3:30 p.m. Only four workdays during the year were recognized as holidays: Fast Day in April, the Fourth of July, Thanksgiving, and Christmas. (Courtesy of Richard Ouellette.)

DANIELSON WORSTED COMPANY. This brick building was built in 1881 for the R. S. Lathrop Company, a manufacturer of reeds used in cotton mills. Starting in 1893, part of the factory was used by H. E. Wilson and Company knitting mill and later still, the Danielson Worsted Company manufactured woolen cloth here. Their business prospered so much during the period of the world wars that the mill was doubled in size. (Courtesy of the Killingly Public Library Archives.)

DANIELSON MANUFACTURING COMPANY. A brick mill was built for Alfred Potter around 1875 in Elmville to replace a frame mill that had occupied the site since at least 1850. It was used by many companies to produce a variety of textiles until 1933, when the Danielson Manufacturing Company, a mill supply manufacturer, moved in. The Danielson Manufacturing Company later diversified and became one of the major suppliers of injection-molded nylon products in the United States.

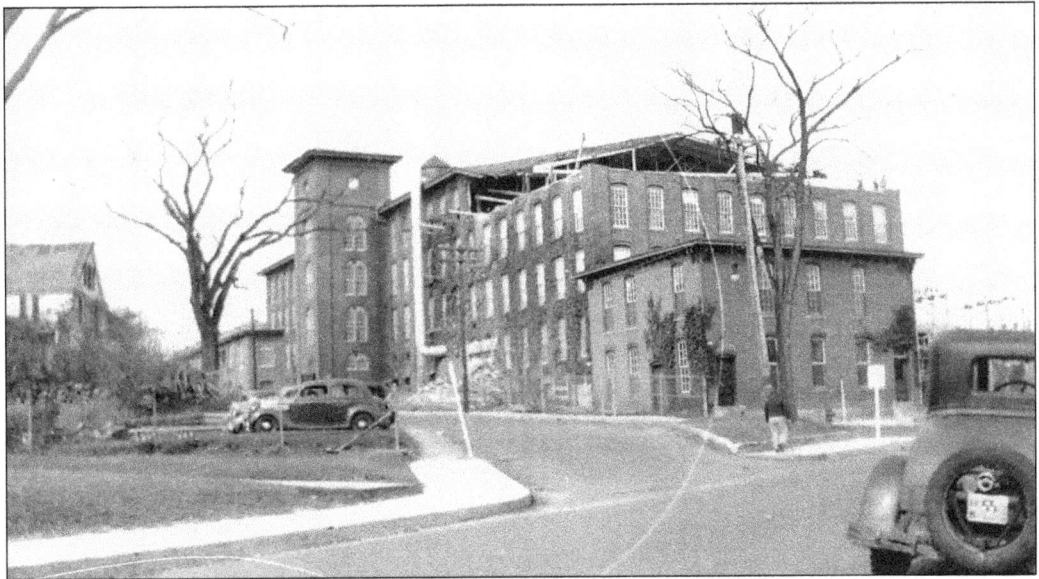

DANIELSON COTTON MILL, 1868. Daniel G. Sherman erected a brick mill on the corner of Main and Maple Streets in Danielsonville. The brick mill replaced a frame cotton mill and two stone mills, which have been destroyed. Shirting and sheeting were manufactured here. In 1925, Powdrell and Alexander took over using the plant for bleaching and weaving. Nearly 160 years of continuous textile production ended in 1963, when the Danielson Finishing Company closed. The photograph above shows extensive damage done to the plant during the great hurricane of September 21, 1938. Below is an aerial view of the mill and surrounding area taken in 1945. (Above, courtesy of Robert J. Coppinger.)

DYER DAM AND POWERHOUSE, 1901–1902. The powerhouse was located south of Danielson on the Quinebaug River. It was owned by the Shoreline Electric Railroad Company to provide the power for the electric railroad (trolley). Its later uses were as a construction company shop, a state highway garage, and a glass company shop. (Courtesy of the McEwen Collection, Killingly Historical and Genealogical Society.)

ELLIOTTVILLE MANUFACTURING COMPANY, EAST KILLINGLY. In 1856, Albert and Lemuel Elliott and Welcome Bartlett formed a stock company, the Elliottville Manufacturing Company, to produce cotton-sheeting cloth. Also located on the Whetstone Brook, the stone structure was built originally in 1833 by Thomas Pray and contained four floors. It grew from 30 looms to 100 looms, 20,000 spindles, and 250 employees.

KNOX GLASS COMPANY, DAYVILLE. During a two week period in July 1957, the people of Killingly accomplished the almost impossible. In order to guarantee that a new industry (the fourth largest manufacturer of glass containers in the United States) would move to the area, the public had to raise $150,000 in 10 days. It would mean a half-million dollar payroll and 150 new jobs that could grow to 250. The Danielson Industrial Foundation took on the challenge and sold the stock within the prescribed time. The dedication of the new facility took place in September 1958. The plant changed ownership several times, becoming Glass Container Corporation in 1978, Diamond-Bathurst, and later Anchor Glass. The photograph was taken November 1964. (Courtesy of Ronald Albee.)

KILNS AT GLASS FACTORY. This is a view of the inside of one of four kilns at Knox Glass in Dayville taken in May 1965. Powdered raw glass entered the kilns, heated to extremely high temperatures, extruded as a bright orange liquid, cut to the length of a bottle, and dropped into a mold to shape the bottle. Because of extremely high temperatures and wear from molten glass moving through it, the kilns had to be rebuilt every three to four years with new fire bricks weighing tons. (Courtesy of Ronald Albee.)

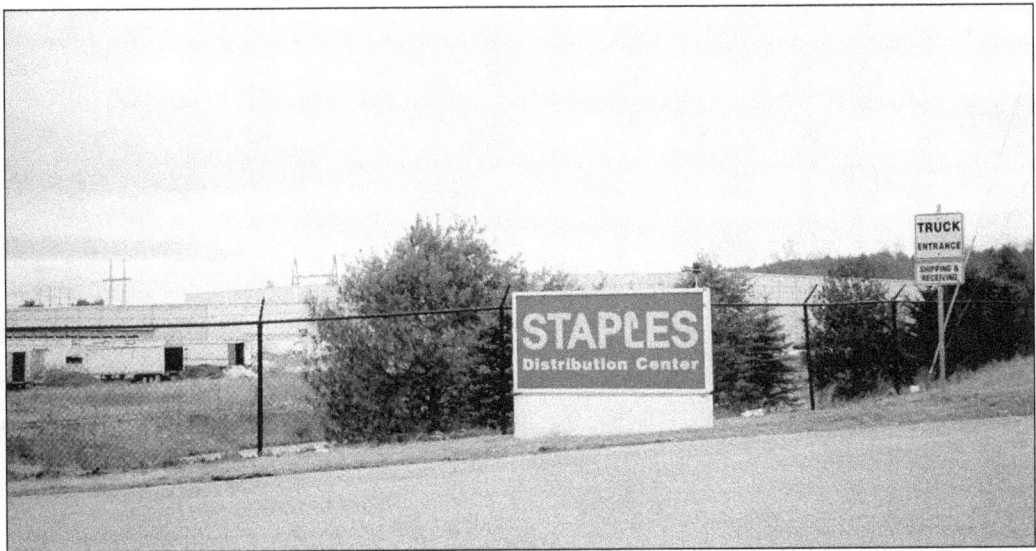

STAPLES DISTRIBUTION NORTHEAST. The home of a Staples distribution center is at 155 Tracy Road in Killingly. Staples is the world's largest office superstore chain. On January 16, 2007, in conjunction with the Connecticut Clean Energy Fund, Staples, and SunEdison, the largest solar power installation in New England, was unveiled here. The solar panels on the roof of this facility have the capacity to produce clean energy to power 14 percent of their energy usage or 36 homes per year.

KILLINGLY INDUSTRIAL PARK. John A. Ricketts, president of the Killingly Industrial Development Corporation, announced plans for the Killingly Industrial Park on November 22, 1975. In June 1976, a $1.5 million federal grant was awarded to Killingly to develop a 158-acre industrial park as 50 percent of the estimated $2.75–3 million cost. There was a potential for 6 to 10 sites that could provide 550–600 jobs according to the town manager. The park proved a success, as all lots have been sold. Plans for an expansion are underway as of 2007. (Courtesy of Virginia Welch.)

LAKE ROAD GENERATING PLANT, DAYVILLE. The new generating plant is located at 56 Alexander Parkway near the Killingly-Putnam town line. The groundbreaking ceremony took place September 23, 1999, with over 200 attending. The grand opening was held June 22, 2002, with over 1,300 in attendance. This is a $490 million project that should generate $55 million in revenues to the Town of Killingly over a period of 20 years. The Lake Road plant supplies power into the ISO New England, a well-established liquid power market. It is a 492-megawatt natural gas–fired plant that is the first in Connecticut after deregulation.

Two

BUSINESSES AND BUILDINGS

In the early days of the town of Killingly, its citizens had to be primarily self-sufficient. The first businesses were the sawmills and gristmills, blacksmiths, and tavern keepers. Gradually from 1835 to 1865, as mills were built and the workers spent long hours at their jobs, a need developed for shops that could provide goods and specialized services such as butchers, grocers, dry goods provisioners, tailors and seamstresses, doctors, and lawyers. There also appeared some strange occupations. Here are just a few—broom man, clicker, gold digger, soap maker, screw peg maker, cigar maker, spool maker, plaster makers, brick maker, sail maker, pen maker, and handkerchief makers.

After the Civil War, Killingly's enormous mills were being built of brick and stone as well as large business blocks in Danielsonville and Daysville. Because the early wooden buildings became victims of fire threatening the entire town, the town fathers passed an ordinance decreeing that all new construction be of brick or stone. The bricks were made and shipped from several brickyards in Dayville, Brooklyn, and Wauregan. Stone was cut from quarries in places such as East Killingly, Breakneck Hill, and Williamsville. Local building materials were also shipped to other towns and cities. During the 1880s, gas streetlights were installed and telephone service started. The Crystal Water Company was chartered in 1883, and in 1893, the first electricity was provided to the town.

The people of the town evidently were too busy in 1808 building and just making a living to hold festivities to observe 100 years of existence; in the summer of 1908, however, the town held its bicentennial with all the buildings draped in red, white, and blue bunting and celebrated with a huge parade.

The town has survived through depressions, wars, and prosperity. Buildings have been torn down and built again. Businesses have come and gone. The following are photographs and information about just a few of them.

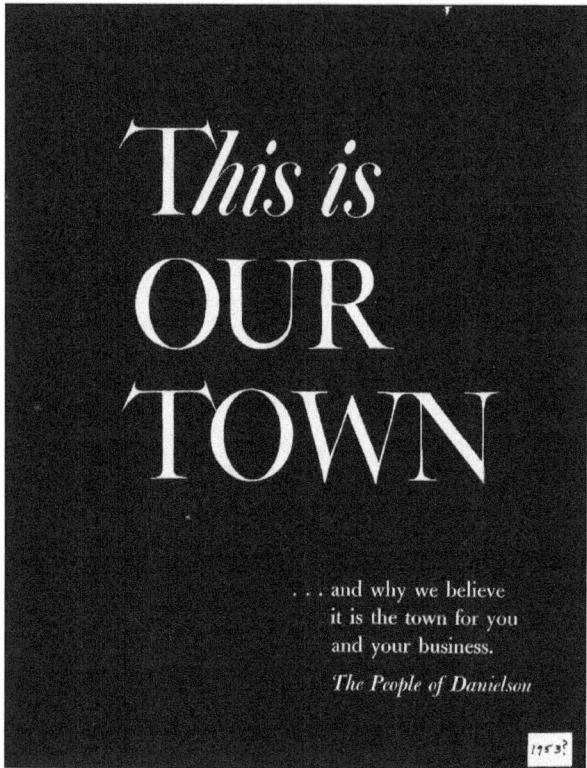

THIS IS OUR TOWN. Pictured is the cover of a booklet published by the Town of Killingly in the late 1950s, when the Danielson Industrial Foundation was actively marketing the town. It contained interviews with folks from various walks of life talking about the advantages of living and working in Killingly. (Courtesy of Richard Ouellette.)

This is
OUR
TOWN

. . . and why we believe
it is the town for you
and your business.

The People of Danielson

1953?

TOWN HALL RENOVATION, DANIELSON. After extensive refurbishing, the town hall was rededicated and an open house was held on January 13, 1985. Back in November 1980, approximately 20 thermal-paned windows had to be custom made to replace windows blasted out by the fire in the Bargain Supply Company building across Main Street. They were installed at a cost of $30,000. (Courtesy of Gilbert Poirier.)

INSIDE MUSIC HALL, DANIELSON. An association of well-to-do citizens had the Music Hall built for $38,000 in 1876. The 800-seat auditorium, stage, and gallery were the site of all types of public entertainment, from operettas to literary readings. The second floor housed the First National Bank of Killingly. Voters cast their ballots in this hall before the use of voting machines. It later became the town hall. (Courtesy of Richard Ouellette.)

DANIELSON SUPERIOR COURT GA11. A view down Center Street in Danielson in November 1998 shows the new superior court under construction, tucked into the hill where the old Danielson Grammar School once stood. Through the girders, the houses on High Street can be seen. The court moved from the town hall into new quarters the first week in July 1999 and held its first new session July 12. (Courtesy of Gilbert Poirier.)

CONNECTICUT STATE POLICE BARRACKS. Troop D state police headquarters was built in 1940 at Westcott Road in Danielson. Roscoe H. Ashley Jr. took this aerial photograph around 1940 from his plane. Note the farms that surrounded the building at that early date. Today's public library would be situated in a large garden patch on the right. The area on the left of the barracks would be the site of the Bonneville's Pharmacy. (Courtesy of Florence Evans.)

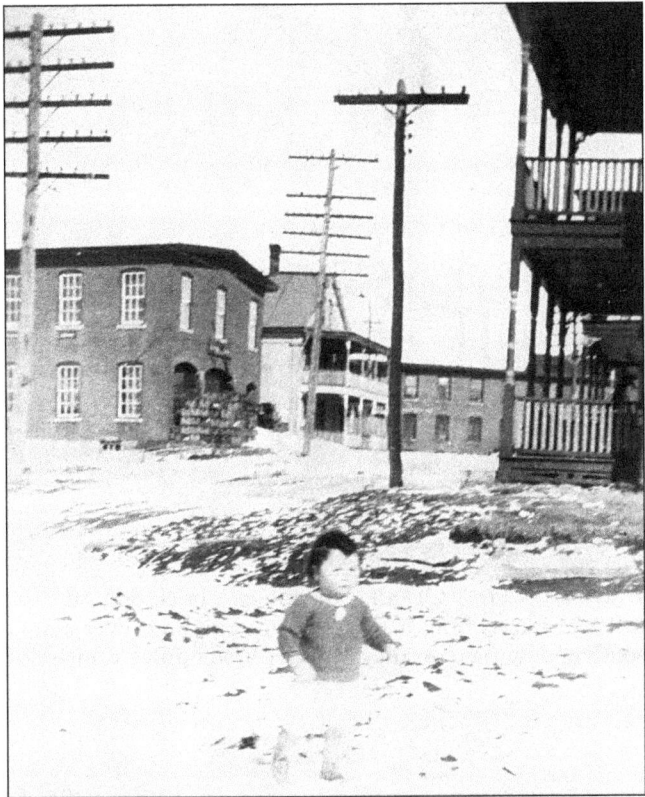

BOROUGH HALL, 1928. In 1868, citizens of the borough of Danielsonville voted to build a brick building on Water Street, 30 by 40 feet, two stories high, for about $3,000 to be used as an engine house, lock up, and for borough meetings. Note the soda crates piled in front of the building. Walter White and Burt Hargraves conducted White's Soda Manufactory in the building from about 1913 to 1928. The child is Augustus Bertorelli. (Courtesy of Patricia Bertorelli Belade.)

KILLINGLY PUBLIC LIBRARY, DANIELSON. In recognition of the need for a larger facility to house the library, ground was broken at the site of the former A&P building on April 19, 1993. Planning started in 1988, and in 1992, the Providence architectural firm of Robinson Green Beretta was selected to design the new building. The library was completed in May and the library moved and reopened in June 1994. The dedication took place October 16, 1994.

DANIELSON POST OFFICE. The village's brick post office was constructed in 1935 ending a long series of moves from a succession of buildings over many, many years. It can be found at the south end of town on the corner of Water and Cottage Streets. (Courtesy of Gilbert Poirier.)

DAYVILLE POST OFFICE. Funny things happen in the post office sometimes. One day in June 1890, a letter was received at the Dayville office addressed to a person in "Hattie Wargon." Of course the postmaster there understood at once that that meant Attawaugan and ensured that it would reach its destination. It might have been a different story today.

BOROUGH FIRE HOUSE, C. 1868. This building housed the fire fighting equipment of the borough. Throughout the town's history, the structure on Water Street has seen many uses. It was a clubhouse for the Polish American Citizens Club, home of the local American Legion post, and turned into a restaurant and club known as the Rain Desert. On December 6, 2007, it opened as The Riverside, a restaurant, bar, and nightspot. (Courtesy of the McEwen Collection, Killingly Historical and Genealogical Society.)

TOWN HALL PARK, DANIELSON. After Wells Mobil Service Station on Main Street was closed, the building was razed to make way for a little park tucked in beside the town hall. The work was done by the Killingly Department of Public Works. There are park benches, trees, shrubbery, flowers, grass, and a walkway for the enjoyment of all. (Courtesy of the Town of Killingly files.)

DANIELSON FIRE STATION. The fire station on the corner of School and Academy Streets was completed in 1908. A fire alarm system for the borough of Danielson was installed at that time. Its dedication took place as part of the town of Killingly's bicentennial celebration. Later an addition housed the borough police department.

36

ATTAWAUGAN FIRE STATION. In July 1959, Attawaugan set up a fire district. The fire districts were for taxing purposes to purchase and maintain firefighting equipment for the companies. The new modern fire station was built in 1981 on Country Club Road in Attawaugan.

DAYVILLE FIRE STATION. Dayville created a fire district in July 1959 to better serve the needs of the village. The new fire station was built in 1977 on Route 12 beside the railroad tracks in the center of Dayville. The industrial park and many other new commercial buildings required more elaborate fire equipment and proper storage for it.

FELSHAW'S TAVERN. The house on the corner of Route 21 and Five Mile River Road on Putnam Heights is one Killingly's oldest taverns. John Felshaw bought Killingly land in 1733, and in 1742 he erected the tavern. It was a well-known spot that was popular with travelers and politicians. Balls were held there as well as court sessions. The militia found it a convenient place to meet on training days.

HARD PAN SHOE STORE. Three generations bought footwear at this store that was established on Railroad Street (now Commerce Avenue) in Danielsonville in 1850 and known by the giant boot out front. Early patrons of the store ordered their handmade boots and shoes to measure. The business was passed from father, William Burrows; to son, William Albert Burrows; and then to son-in-law, Sidney H. Perry. (Courtesy of the Gertrude Pradel Collection, Killingly Historical and Genealogical Society.)

K. A. DARBIE FURNITURE. Kent A. Darbie was connected with Bacon's furniture and coffin rooms for many years. He went into business in 1884 upholstering furniture and picture framing, later adding a new line in the form of wallpapers. He also handled stoves and ranges. This was his delivery truck. (Courtesy of Joseph Chauvin.)

HENRY A. MYERS. Henry A. Meyers started his business career in 1912 with a horse and cart. After serving in World War I, Myers built the original store on Mechanics Street. He was the first in Danielson to put in a commercial refrigeration plant and install a milk pasteurization plant. He enlarged his store three times, the last in 1959. Myers died in March 1962, only two weeks after retiring. (Courtesy of Joseph Chauvin.)

FORMER METHODIST PARSONAGE, c. 1873. The Main Street, Danielsonville, business block in the former Methodist Church Parsonage burned about 1892 and later was rebuilt. Pictured is the fruit store of Ignatius Longo around 1900. For more than 20 years starting in 1934, it housed Samuel and Sadie Goodman's women's wearing apparel shop, the Boston Store, as well as several other businesses. By 1979, only a vacant lot remained. (Courtesy of the McEwen Collection, Killingly Historical and Genealogical Society.)

FRANKLIN BUILDING, DANIELSONVILLE. Horace Davis and Charles Blackmar constructed the two-story brick building in 1855 known as the Davis Block on Main Street. The *Transcript* printers located there in 1861, and in 1866 the owner rechristened it the Franklin Building because many associated printing with Benjamin Franklin. W. O. Jacobs and Company hardware store served customers here for many years. (Courtesy of Richard Ouellette.)

KEYSTONE STORE. Before its move to the lower end of Main Street, Walter Dixon's Keystone Store was in the Franklin Building on the corner of Main and Center Streets. Henry Herman, the tailor, was in the small shop next door in 1908. The shops were patriotically decorated for Killingly's bicentennial celebration. (Courtesy of the McEwen Collection, Killingly Historical and Genealogical Society.)

SAVINGS BANK BUILDING, DANIELSON, 1866. Windham County Savings Bank was organized in 1864 and conducted business through the early years of the 20th century. G. W. Nash, the Music Man's store was in this building on Main Street; he also led an orchestra. Occupants in the 1940s and 1950s were two grocery stores and a shoe store. Later it housed a jewelry store, beauty shop, law offices, and an insurance company. (Courtesy of the McEwen Collection, Killingly Historical and Genealogical Society.)

YOUNG BROTHERS COMPANY, MECHANIC STREET, DANIELSON. Cosmer A. Young's brother, William J. Young, joined him in the coal and lumber business soon after he started in 1887. The firm became Young Brothers Company. When he first started, he solicited orders for coal in the morning, ate his lunch at the office at noon, and delivered the coal with his one horse and wagon in the afternoon. (Courtesy of Joseph Chauvin.)

Danielson, Conn., *Nov 20* 190 *2*

M *iss Jane Perkins*

BOUGHT OF The Peoples Ice Co.,

DEALERS IN

QUINEBAUG LAKE ICE ONLY.

TELEPHONE, 18-12.

June	2	185	the 2	a 25	46
July	1	680	"	"	1 70
July	1	660	"	"	1 65
Sept	1	710	"	"	1 78
Oct	1	525	"	"	1 32
Nov	1	570	"	"	1 43	8 34
		Jan 25		Paid in full	

PEOPLE'S ICE COMPANY. One Sunday afternoon in 1914 many took advantage of the clear sky and bracing air and hurried to Quinebaug Lake. There, 40–50 men engaged in harvesting fine quality nine-inch ice. Under the supervision of Charles S. Francis, the work went merrily on. The mark set by the ice company as their quota was 4,000 tons of ice. (Courtesy of the Jane Frances Perkins Collection, Killingly Historical and Genealogical Society.)

WINKELMAN SHOE STORE. J. W. Winkelman, who was born in Germany, began his business in Danielsonville in 1877. He moved to this location on Main Street in 1888, selling shoes, boots, hosiery, leather, and findings. Next door was the shop of W. J. Craig, the Irish tailor, who conducted his business there from 1898 to 1920. He died in 1954. (Courtesy of the McEwen Collection, Killingly Historical and Genealogical Society.)

GROCERY STORE INTERIOR. The employees are, from left to right, unidentified, ? St. Laurent, Joseph W. Friese, Albert Nash, and Henry Bodo, manager. They worked in the First National Store on Main Street that was in the LaClair Building. Note how all the merchandise is mostly behind the counters where only the clerks have access to it. (Courtesy of Joseph Chauvin.)

LAW OFFICES. The two buildings on Academy Street in Danielson were built around 1875 as dwellings. In 1917, Martin Burns converted the one on the left to a funeral parlor now occupied by attorneys Thomas DuPont and James Scheibler. Dr. Frank P. Todd used the building on the right as his home and office. In 1950, Ralph Koski opened a bakery in it, followed by Sylvio Gauthier and John Tewksbury. A realtor preceded the law offices of Gail Rooke-Norman. (Courtesy of Gilbert Poirier.)

A. LONGO FRUIT STORE, C. 1910. Situated at 85 Main Street in Danielson, the store was owned by Augustus Longo who was born in Fermini, Sicily, in 1868. His wife, Annie, became proprietor some time in the 1920s. She is pictured here with three of her children, Michael, Joseph, and Antonia. (Courtesy of Nicholas A. Longo.)

44

LOWER MAIN STREET, DANIELSON, LATE 1930s. Main Street in downtown Danielson was a busy time in the 1930s. On the right were the A&P Store and Downyflake Doughnuts. On the left were the Star Bakery, Boston Meat Market, Danielson Fruit Company, Charon's Department Store, Keech's Department Store, Bonneville's Pharmacy, a Shell station, and Reeve's Gulf Station. (Courtesy of the Gertrude Pradel Collection, Killingly Historical and Genealogical Society.)

GEORGE JENCKS, HARDWARE, TIN, AND STOVE STORE. George Jencks, age 25, came to Danielsonville in 1879 and started a stove and tinware business. After partnering with J. Horace Jones, they added hardware to their stock. His business was originally in Crandall's Block on Railroad Square but moved to the Dexter Block on Main Street in Danielsonville in 1884. He also had a cart on the road to sell his wares. (Courtesy of Richard Ouellette.)

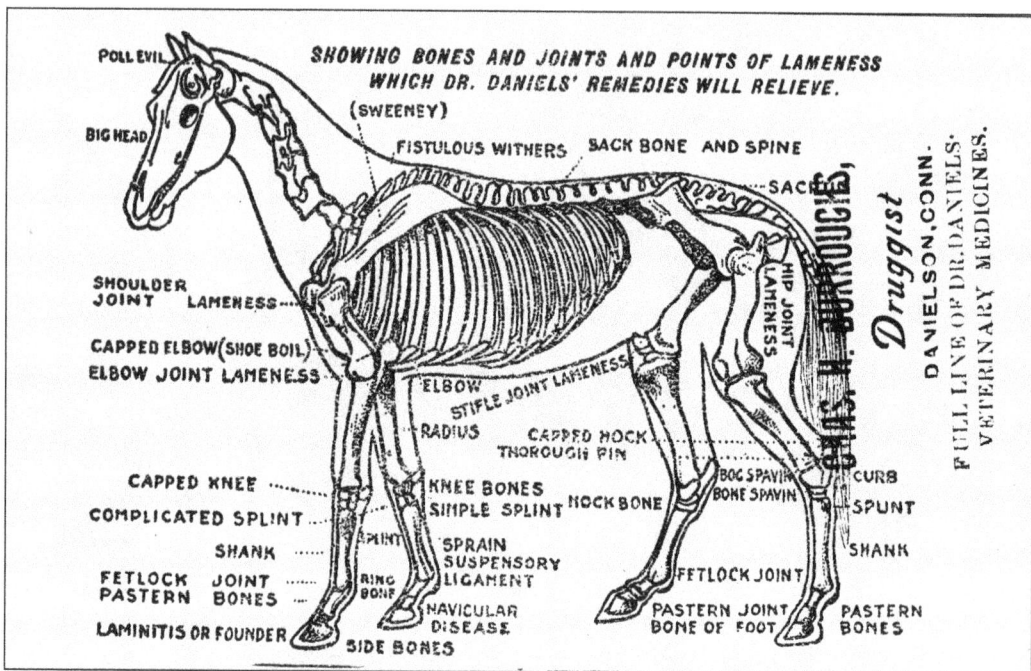

SHOWING BONES AND JOINTS AND POINTS OF LAMENESS WHICH DR. DANIELS' REMEDIES WILL RELIEVE.

POLL EVIL

BIG HEAD

(SWEENEY)

FISTULOUS WITHERS   SACK BONE AND SPINE

SACR...

SHOULDER JOINT LAMENESS

CAPPED ELBOW (SHOE BOIL)
ELBOW JOINT LAMENESS

HIP JOINT LAMENESS

ELBOW
STIFLE JOINT LAMENESS
RADIUS   CAPPED HOCK
THOROUGH PIN

CAPPED KNEE
COMPLICATED SPLINT
SHANK
FETLOCK JOINT
PASTERN BONES
LAMINITIS OR FOUNDER

KNEE BONES
SIMPLE SPLINT   HOCK BONE
SPLINT
SPRAIN
SUSPENSORY
LIGAMENT
RING BONE
NAVICULAR
DISEASE
SIDE BONES

BOG SPAVIN
BONE SPAVIN

CURB
SPUNT
SHANK

FETLOCK JOINT

PASTERN JOINT
BONE OF FOOT

PASTERN BONES

CHAS. H. BURROUGHS, *Druggist* DANIELSON, CONN.
FULL LINE OF DR. DANIELS' VETERINARY MEDICINES.

BUSINESS CARD OF CHARLES H. BURROUGHS, DRUGGIST. Charles H. Burroughs began work in 1867 at age 16 in the drug store of R. F. Lyon in Danielson. In 1897, he became an equal partner with Lyon and became owner upon Lyon's death. When Burroughs died in 1906, he had been in the pharmacy business for 39 years. (Courtesy of Richard Ouellette.)

EXCHANGE BLOCK. Burroughs operated the drug store on Main Street in Danielson in 1901, which had been run earlier by Lyon. The barbershop was Mr. Healey's, and later Gaston Maindon's. The last store on the far end was Armington's grocery. The Masonic lodge used the third floor, and Girl Scouts met on the second floor in the early 1900s. The third floor hall was used by the Daughters of Isabella around 1940. (Courtesy of the McEwen Collection, Killingly Historical and Genealogical Society.)

46

ADAMS EXPRESS COMPANY AND A. F. WOOD LIVERY AND STABLE, C. 1903. The Adams Express started in business in the mid-1800s on Railroad Square in Danielson. Henry Holt Starkweather acted as agent there for 38 years from 1882. A. F. Wood purchased the O. W. Bowen livery business November 7, 1902, and made it the best-equipped stable in the vicinity. He also owned an undertaking business. (Courtesy of the Killingly Public Library Archives.)

CHARLES H. PELLETT LIVERY. Charles Pellett operated several businesses over the years. Besides the Danielson Garage, he owned a livery, feed, and sale stable at 7 Furnace Street in Danielson in the early part of the 20th century. By 1923, he had moved to 221 Main Street and was selling and servicing new Hudson and Essex automobiles and used cars. (Courtesy of Dorothy Hutchins Pryor.)

47

OBSERVER PRINTING SHOP. At the end of the 19th century Dayville had a newspaper known as the *Observer Review*. Nathan W. Kennedy was the editor and Frank P. White was the business manager. The building was located next door to the Dayville Hotel on Main Street. The newspaper was printed from 1898 to about 1900.

STEAM ENGINE TRAIN. Behind the beautiful, big steam locomotive is the Dayville Hotel in this photograph taken some time in the 1870s or 1880s. Sayles Hall, the building directly behind the hotel, was called the Opera House according to an older resident of Dayville.

DAYVILLE HOTEL. The hotel was built prior to 1855 with Horace Woodard as the proprietor. L. M. Kennedy, the proprietor in 1874, had piazzas built on the front and east sides extending to the first and second stories. It fronted on the railroad tracks near the depot. The new firm of Kennedy and Young totally renovated in 1889 and celebrated with a free supper and dance. It was torn down about 1949–1950.

WILDWOOD PARK HOUSE, DAYVILLE, C. 1871. Luther Alexander built a summer boarding house situated on beautiful Alexander's Lake in a lovely pine grove. People came to this summer resort from many sections of the country. He also planned for a small steamboat and sailing craft on the lake and numerous other attractions. In the 1880s, the proprietors were C. H. Bassett and C. F. Cobb. (Courtesy of Henry Hopkins.)

GINGRAS GARAGE, DAYVILLE. Alfred J. Gingras operated his garage in the 1920s and 1930s as well as offering a livery and automobile rental service. Close scrutiny will reveal that the price on the gasoline pump says 15.9¢ per gallon. From 1945 to July 1969, it was run by Stanley S. Barstow as Barstow Transportation's garage and later moved to Mechanics Street in Danielson. Barstow sold the Dayville property to Danielson Oil Company. The building became the home of Bissonnette's Car Wash.

DOWE BUILDING, 1927. Once the home of one of the oldest businesses in Danielson, the Dowe Building on Main Street has also housed the Smart Shoppe, a women's clothing store, and on the second floor, there was a beauty shop, a barbershop, and an insurance agency. Dowe's started business in 1854 and remained family-owned until 1967 when the building and business were purchased by Robert and Lucille Trahan. Announcement of the store's closing was made December 31, 2003, by the owner at that time, Randy Daggett. Below, the merchant's card of John Marshall Dowe advertised his picture framing business. He not only ran the stationery and newspaper stand but was also the comptroller of the State of Connecticut at the time of his death at age 49 on May 15, 1946. (Above, courtesy of Gilbert Poirier; below, courtesy of Richard Ouellette.)

JOHN M. DOWE,
Dealer in
PICTURE FRAMES !
DANIELSONVILLE, CONN.

NEW YORK FRUIT STORE. G. Malucelli and Louis Bertorelli, both from Bardy, Italy, founded the New York Fruit Store on October 20, 1890, in the Phoenix Building on Main Street in Danielson. Malucelli was the candy maker, and Bertorelli was the ice cream maker. In 1913, Mary Salotti succeeded them. Bertorelli became sole owner in 1928. The store handled fruit, candy, nuts, groceries, ice cream, tobacco, and cigarettes. Augustus Bertorelli is shown below, inside the store. Thousands of youngsters stopped in over the years to purchase their penny candy before the movies. Who can forget the "black cows" (otherwise known as root beer floats) that were served in the ice cream parlor at the rear of the store? (Courtesy of Patricia Bertorelli Belade.)

SUNSHINE CARD SHOP, DANIELSON.
F. Raymond Lemieux posed with his Overland automobile in front of the Sunshine Card Shop. He originally started with a printing shop while his father, F. X. Lemieux, sold cards and operated a lending library for a small fee per day. (Courtesy of Marguerite Dumaine.)

INTERIOR OF SUNSHINE CARD SHOP. One of Danielson's best known stores was in the 1919 Davis Building on Main Street. F. X. Lemieux established the business in September 1932 for the purpose of "scattering sunshine with greeting cards and gifts." F. Raymond Lemieux managed the store for many years, and later F. X. Lemieux's granddaughter, Marguerite, and her husband, Robert Dumaine, carried on the family tradition. The business closed August 31, 1998. (Courtesy of Marguerite Dumaine.)

FIRE IN KEYSTONE BLOCK, DANIELSON. At 2:30 a.m. on January 9, 1970, a devastating fire left 12 persons homeless and several businesses wiped out. Buddy's Tavern, Ye Old Washboard self-service laundry, Bargain Supply Company, and Pete's Lunch were involved as well as a vacant store last occupied by Red Carpet Grill. Seven other fire companies responded to a mutual aid call and three companies were on standby. Near-zero temperatures turned the water streaming from the hoses into ice almost as soon as it hit the air. The thick wall of ice that accumulated between the Keystone and Pete's Lunch protected it from the fire, causing only broken windows and some water damage. The damage ran as high as $100,000. The building was approximately 65 years old and was owned by Harry and Theodore Evergates. (Courtesy of George and Demeter Lakatsis.)

GEORGE'S GALLEY. George and Demeter (Fafaras) Lakatzis built their restaurant in 1978 on the site of the block destroyed by fire in 1970. They carried on the reputation of excellent food her father, Peter Fafaras, and Peter Kalivas had enjoyed at Pete's Lunch since 1947. Other businesses in the old block were Vandale's News, Sunshine Card Shop, Baton's Coffee Shop, and Keystone Department Store. (Courtesy of George and Demeter Lakatsis.)

EVANS BLOCK, 1878. The building was constructed on Main Street in Danielsonville by Thomas J. Evans in 1879. The 26-by-30-foot block was built for the sum of $16,000. Fire severely damaged the building in 1880, but it was repaired. It has housed a millinery shop, restaurant, variety store, package store, upholstery shop, water bed shop, and a gift shop named Heart and Home, as well as other businesses. (Courtesy of George and Demeter Lakatsis.)

DANIELSON, AERIAL VIEW, C. LATE 1800S. This photograph gives a bird's-eye view of Danielson from the lower end of Main Street. The Keystone Building is in the lower center. Note the two church spires in the upper left—the early Methodist church on the left and the Westfield Congregational Church on the right. The house on the lower right is Hannah

Bennett's millinery shop. It originally was the office of Dr. Samuel Hutchins from some time before 1845. Bennett remodeled it into a millinery store. She advertised beautiful styles of silk, lawn, and straw bonnets. Emelaide Upham purchased the business in 1866, later selling to Miss E. Raymond and Mrs. G. M. Clarke. By 1881, its use had been changed to a fish market.

THE TRINKET SHOPPE, DANIELSON. The building was constructed in 1846 by Luther Day and is one of the oldest in continuous commercial use in Danielson. It is on the corner of Main and Union Streets and is now home of the Trinket Shoppe, which was established in 1970 by Don and Barbara Vachon. It has expanded several times to take in the whole block, plus the block next to it. (Courtesy of Gilbert Poirier.)

DANIELSON SURPLUS STORE, DANIELSON. The Bradley Building was built around 1903. About 1908 it was occupied by a men's clothing store called Hurlbut's. The Danielson Trust Company was later accommodated there. It housed a Rexall Pharmacy for many years. On May 20, 1955, David and Shirley Rosenburg, owners of Danielson Surplus Sales, established in 1950, moved to this new location. It continues today with their son Warren in charge. (Courtesy of Gilbert Poirier.)

SOUTHERN NEW ENGLAND TELEPHONE COMPANY. Telephone service started in Danielsonville in 1882. First called Connecticut Telephone Company, it became Southern New England Telephone Company in October 1882 and located here, until they moved into a new building on Main Street in 1942. The structure on the corner of Mechanic and Academy Streets became the printing plant of the *Windham County Transcript* in April 1954. It was torn down in April 1960. (Courtesy of the McEwen Collection, Killingly Historical and Genealogical Society.)

COLT'S PLASTICS' OFFICE, ELMVILLE. In 1979, Colt's Plastics Company moved to this office and mill, which formerly belonged to Danielson Manufacturing Company. Colt's Plastics Company began as a subsidiary of Colt Firearms in Hartford in the 1920s to manufacture plastic caps such as toothpaste tube caps. They now design and manufacture jar packaging systems primarily for the cosmetic, pharmaceutical, and personal care industries. (Courtesy of the McEwen Collection, Killingly Historical and Genealogical Society.)

TILLINGHAST FUNERAL HOME. The house on the corner of Academy and Mechanics Streets in Danielson was the home of Waldo Tillinghast and his family. The ell facing Mechanics Street was the Tillinghast Funeral Parlor. Tillinghast succeeded A. F. Wood in 1937. The business was moved to 202 Main Street in Danielson early in the 1960s and later taken over by Waldo's son Craig Tillinghast. (Courtesy of the McEwen Collection, Killingly Historical and Genealogical Society.)

CROSBY'S GREENHOUSE, ACADEMY STREET, DANIELSON. The floral business was established early in 1900 and stayed in the Crosby family until about 1937. Several owners followed including Eric Larson, Theodore Fisher, George and John Balfour, and Rochelle Fiske. (Courtesy of the McEwen Collection, Killingly Historical and Genealogical Society.)

ZIP'S DINER, DAYVILLE. Henry "Zip" Zehrer was the owner of the diner at the junction of Routes 101 and 12 in Dayville in 1954. In later years, Conrad Jodoin ran the business, and at present, it is owned by his son Thomas Jodoin. It is a popular eatery and a favorite gathering place for morning coffee. There was a gala celebration in 2004 to celebrate their 50th anniversary.

LUKE'S COFFEE SHOP. Luke O. and Mabel O. Gendreau established the coffee shop at 106 Main Street in Danielson on December 8, 1945. Mabel can be seen in the background. Mrs. Despathie is the customer. It was named for its owner and continued in business until the mid-1950s.

61

DANIELSON OIL COMPANY. Richard Banigan established a filling station and bulk depot on Railroad Street in Danielson in October 1927, distributing Sinclair products. In 1945, Edward Cunneen, Norman Davignon, and Deforest Wells Jr. became officers of the corporation that then distributed Shell products. A new office building was constructed in 1950 on the site of the old Hard Pan Shoe Store. (Courtesy of Richard Ouellette.)

EARLY DINER. Every town had a diner. Danielson's was called Duffy's Diner for at least 20 years during the 1940s and 1950s and was operated by Helen Duffy and later Rosario Benoit. In the 1960s, it was known as Marie's Diner. The menu changed drastically in 1973 when it was opened as the Egg Roll King featuring a full Chinese food menu as well as American food. (Courtesy of Gilbert Poirier.)

HILLTOP SERVICE STATION, C. 1940. Allen Moffit stands beside the gas pumps at his gas station on the southeast corner of Route 101 and Bailey Hill Road in East Killingly. Earlier it had been run by N. Allen Wade. In 1953, Walter M. Shippee owned and operated the little station.

BONNEVILLE'S PHARMACY, DANIELSON. Bonneville's Pharmacy opened the doors of its new building on Westcott Road near the state police barracks in August 1977. Owned by Richard Harrison, the larger facility offered new departments and health care items. Bonneville's Pharmacy moved from its former Main Street location, where it was a downtown Danielson landmark for 76 years. For about 10 years in the 1980s, Dr. Clifford Farmer, a chiropodist, had his office there. (Courtesy of Gilbert Poirier.)

T. H. Ray and Kennedy Corporation. T. H. Ray started his business in June 1935 with one tank truck. The 1936 purchase of a metered truck and 1943 installation of ticket printing meters were the first in Danielson. The gas station and bulk plant at the corner of Cottage and Furnace Streets were leased in 1945. The Kennedy Corporation lumber and coal yard is across the street. (Courtesy of Joseph Chauvin.)

T. H. Ray Station and Coffee Shop. In 1955, T. H. Ray Heating Oils held an open house in their new headquarters on North Main Street in Danielson. A lunchroom known as Ray's Coffee Shop was operated by Ernest Boston. The business employed 14 people that included Gerry Leonard, Robert Baranski, Walter "Sarge" Chauvin, Leo Lafave, Ray Choquette, Cecelia Ray, and Alice Caffrey. (Courtesy of Joseph Chauvin.)

BARGAIN SUPPLY COMPANY. Harold S. Blumenthal moved his plumbing and electrical supply business from 30 Main Street to 128 Main Street in Danielson due to a destructive fire at the former address on January 9, 1970. Ironically he was again the victim of a devastating fire on March 7, 1980, that caused the loss of three buildings and seven businesses totaling close to $500,000. Nearly 150 firefighters from 12 departments in the 10-town region helped battle the flames for almost 18 hours. (Courtesy of Gilbert Poirier.)

MALLOY'S FAMILY DEPARTMENT STORE. The grand opening of Malloy's Family Department Store on Main Street in Danielson was held March 24, 1976, in a building previously built for W. T. Grant Company. Diskay Discount store took the place of W. T. Grant in 1971, followed by Malloy's Family Department Store, which remained open for about 10 years. A variety of businesses have been there since then, including an appliance store, computer store, and a recruiting office. (Courtesy of Gilbert Poirier.)

SUNNY LUNCH RESTAURANT. The popular restaurant established July 25, 1930, on Center Street in Danielson, derived its name from the "sunny side of the street." Past owners were Alton Frost, Tyler Andrews, Henry Briere, Aunt Susie Hopkins, George McKeone, and Antonio Caron. In 1934, during a national textile strike, they fed the militia. Employees of utilities companies were served during floods in 1937 and at the time of the 1938 hurricane. (Courtesy of Gilbert Poirier.)

PHOENIX HALL BLOCK, 1894. The Phoenix Hall building on Center Street in Danielson had a large store on the first floor and the Phoenix Theatre on the second for many years. Burroughs and Hopkins did the printing of the *Windham County Transcript* here all through its changes of ownership. In the 1920s, the theater was known as the Majestic. In 1979, the Benevolent and Protective Order of Elks purchased the building. (Courtesy of Gilbert Poirier.)

BEAUTY SHOP, C. 1935. In 1939, 24–28 Center Street in Danielson was an upholstery shop. The ell in the rear probably was a *c.* 1920 garage and an even earlier blacksmith shop. It could possibly have been the site of a carriage painting business. Since about 1960, it has been the home of, first, Evelyn's Beauty Shop, and then Magic Mirror. Recently it has been a delicatessen. (Courtesy of Gilbert Poirier.)

PHIL'S RADIO. The Woodis Oyster House and Restaurant, formerly known as Kennedy's Restaurant, was in the former Graham Building on Main Street in Danielsonville. In the 1890s, it was operated by C. H. Woodis. It is believed that the building was built about 1850 as the tailor shop of Daniel E. Hill, and then housed James K. Logee's Bakery. Later it was a cigar store, fruit store, confectionery, and then Phil's Radio. (Courtesy of Gilbert Poirier.)

DONUT KETTLE, DANIELSON. From 1868 on, this building on Main Street was the drugstore of W. W. Woodward, who sold not only medicines and tobacco, but also chemicals, acids, dyes, paints, oils, and varnishes. It operated under the name W. W. Woodward's Drug Store from 1868 to the mid-1960s. Since that time it has been occupied by a number of businesses, such as the Donut Kettle, Belade's, Andy's Pizza, and others. (Courtesy of Gilbert Poirier.)

PHOENIX BLOCK, DANIELSON, 1896. The Phoenix Block originally accommodated the First National Bank of Killingly and the Windham County National Bank. Space was rented to an organ salesroom and the New York Fruit Store. The block includes five stores and seven offices. Other stores have included Lord's Shoe Store, Henry McEwen's Jewelry Store, Alan Clothes, A. E. Meech Hardware, Sherwin Williams Company, Pierre Boulaine Fancy Groceries, and Specialty Fruit Store. (Courtesy of Gilbert Poirier.)

SEARS, ROEBUCK AND COMPANY. Sears constructed new quarters on Furnace Street in Danielson in 1965, replacing a building that once housed a laundromat and barbershop. It was aligned with the next building, Danielson Remnant and Novelty Company, originally Louis E. Kennedy's Undertaking and Livery Stable for 48 years, dating from 1895. Rose's Mini Mart moved into part of the Sears building, and Steve Bousquet's Appliance and Television replaced Sears. (Courtesy of Gilbert Poirier.)

HURME RADIO AND OTHER SHOPS, C. 1860. The building complex has been the home of Hurme's Radio since 1949, established by Birger and Armi Hurme, sold to Richard and Helen Gaudreau in 1963, and later sold to their son Michael in 2000. Over the years, other portions of the building have served as a tin shop, carpentry shop, paint shop, package store, barbershop, and credit bureau. (Courtesy of Gilbert Poirier.)

VIP CATALOG SHOWROOM. A new business facility opened August 8, 1973, owned by Louis and Richard Legare. The building was owned by Louis Siegel, who operated Lavallee Furniture Company here for about 40 years. VIP was a new concept in merchandising, offering a showroom of goods with distributor prices. Buster Mahoney's later occupied the site on Commerce Avenue before being razed in 2000 to make Water Street a through street. (Courtesy of Gilbert Poirier.)

KEYSTONE CLEANERS. Although considerably modernized, this commercial building dates back to about 1870. A number of businesses have sheltered under its roof from Surprise Dry Goods Store; a "Yankee Notions" shop; several clothing stores, including Blue Front Clothing Store and People's Clothing Store; Adrian Poirier's barbershop; Keystone Cleaners; and presently, a kitchen supply store called the Kitchen Witch. (Courtesy of Gilbert Poirier.)

GIL'S SHOE BARN. The store occupying the Diamond Block on Main Street in Danielson was the site of the business owned by Palmer C. Sherman and James E. Keech that was purchased in 1927 by Sam Florman and called Keech's Department Store. Gilbert J. and Elizabeth Poirier acquired the business in 1965, and by 1971, it was called Keech's Mini Mall. It housed Gil's Shoe Barn, which is now owned by Gilbert's daughter, Debbie Halback. (Courtesy of Gilbert Poirier.)

LONGO BLOCK. The old Longo Block on Main Street in Danielson, the site of Longo Fruit Store in 1907, was damaged by fire and rebuilt in 1924. Alice Eleanor shop moved there from the Diamond Block in 1925 and remained until 1996. It was again damaged by fire in 1968 and 1972. Other businesses located there were Morin's Pharmacy, Allard's Pharmacy, Nash's Fruit Store, Cloutier's Delicatessen, and the Sanctuary. (Courtesy of Gilbert Poirier.)

SPINNING WHEEL GIFT SHOP, DANIELSON. This building on Main Street, around 1870, accommodated a grocery store owned by the Danielson Company and remained mill property through the 1930s. Johnnie's Market was established there in 1939 until 1964. Eatmore Lunch occupied part of the building for some 20 years from the 1940s to the 1960s. The Spinning Wheel and Kathy's Koiffures started in 1978 and lasted until the early 1990s. The building was later torn down. (Courtesy of Gilbert Poirier.)

MAIN STREET BUSINESSMEN, C. 1988. The group of business people organized to promote shopping in Downtown Danielson gathered for a Christmas photograph. It was taken in the gazebo in Davis Park on Main Street. In this photograph are people representing retail stores, a restaurant, an oil company, a bank, a travel agency, and a glass company. (Courtesy of Ted Aubin.)

HOLIDAY INN EXPRESS, DAYVILLE. The first major hotel chain to establish a presence in Windham County opened the doors of its latest hotel in July 1999, just off Interstate 395 at exit 94 near Killingly's Industrial Park. There are 78 rooms, of which 17 are suites. The hotel also has a pool and an exercise room.

LAUREL HOUSE RESTAURANT. The restaurant and banquet center adjacent to the Holiday Inn Express at 8 Tracy Road in Dayville opened to the public October 29, 1999, for lunch and dinner. It added to the commercial presence in that section of Killingly. It was sold and, as of April 2007, it is the Gold Eagle Restaurant owned by Peter J. Malcoon.

GOLDEN GREEK, ATTAWAUGAN. Built by restaurateurs Nicholas Thanas, George Gionis, and Richard Burke in 1982, the restaurant is one of a number of top-notch eateries in the Killingly area. This one is on Route 12 and boasts a sunroom as well as the regular dining room areas.

WILLIMANTIC TRUST COMPANY, DANIELSON. County Bank and Trust Company on Main Street and the Willimantic Trust Company merged in 1967. They opened a branch office in Dayville in 1970. The building was completely renovated in 1975. After several more mergers ending with Fleet Bank, it was purchased by the Citizens National Bank of Putnam. The Northeastern Connecticut Chamber of Commerce office is on the second floor of the Main Street office. (Courtesy of Gilbert Poirier.)

DANIELSON FEDERAL SAVINGS AND LOAN ASSOCIATION, 1960. The bank was established in 1916, occupying the Evergates Building until their move to 142 Main Street in Danielson in October 1960 with a grand opening celebration. In 1975, a branch opened inside Barker's Department Store in Dayville, which at that time was only the second bank of that type in New England. New London Trust took over in 1997, Westbank in 2006, and New Alliance in 2007.

CONNECTICUT BANK AND TRUST COMPANY. This bank is the result of many mergers over the years. It started life as Windham County National Bank in 1822. Later it became the Hartford-Connecticut Trust Company, then the Connecticut Bank and Trust Company in 1955. They moved into this new building on Main Street in Danielson in 1963. Since that time, there have been more mergers with Fleet Bank and later Bank of America.

SITE OF FUTURE KILLINGLY COMMONS. Site work is beginning on the former Anchor Glass property near exit 93 of Interstate 395 and Route 101 in Dayville to prepare it for the construction of a new shopping center. After Anchor Glass closed in 1997, the property sat idle for eight years. Extensive environmental remedial cleanup had to be completed on the contaminated site before the development for this new use of 525,000 square feet of stores.

THE GASTON-HOVEY HOUSE, C. 1790. On the northeast corner of Halls Hill and Cook Hill Roads sits the oldest house in the South Killingly hilltop village. Alexander Gaston, a prominent merchant, acquired it in 1802. Gaston sold the dwelling to Dr. Daniel Hovey, a respected physician in the community, in 1838. It was willed to the South Killingly Congregational Church in 1912 for use as a parsonage. (Courtesy of the McEwen Collection, Killingly Historical and Genealogical Society.)

PROVIDENCE AND DANIELSON TROLLEY. Construction began on People's Tramway line between Danielson and Putnam in 1901. The Providence and Danielson line was constructed in 1902–1903. A waiting station was erected in Elmville where the line connected with the People's Tramway. The distance from Providence to Danielson by trolley was 35 miles and the fare was 50¢. The running time for that trip was three hours.

TROLLEY PASSING DAVIS PARK. J. Q. A. Stone, editor of the *Windham County Transcript*, spearheaded a movement in 1890 to raise money to buy land from the estate of Capt. Samuel Reynolds for a park. Altogether $6,000 was raised. The largest individual gift was from Edwin W. Davis, a former Danielson resident. Davis requested that the park be named in memory of his parents, Randall and Philia Kies Davis. (Courtesy of Thomas Guillemette.)

Three

CHURCHES, SCHOOLS, AND CEMETERIES

The original township of Killingly included the present towns of Thompson, Killingly, and nearly all of Putnam. The first church was located to the east of Route 21, a little south of the present Killingly-Putnam town line and on the same side as the present Putnam Heights meetinghouse. Early life in the town revolved closely around the church societies. The Separatist Church of South Killingly was organized in 1746. The Church of West Killingly was built in 1796 and was followed by the Methodist, St. James Catholic, St. Alban's Episcopal, Adventist Christian, Baptist, and Nazarene churches. Churches in the other villages were the Attawaugan Methodist church, the Church of the Five Wounds (St. Anne's) in Ballouville, Dayville Congregational and St. Joseph's Catholic Churches, East Killingly Baptist and Free Will Baptist Churches, as well as Our Lady of Peace Catholic Church and the Williamsville Congregational that later became St. Ignatius Catholic Church in Rogers.

Schools were given important consideration by the town. In 1869, Killingly was divided into 15 school districts. After World War II, the first priority of the town was to rebuild the Goodyear School that had burned in 1945. That school was completed in 1948, and the Killingly Center School closed. An increase in population made it necessary for three schools to go on double sessions. Killingly Memorial School in Danielson was completed in 1952; Danielson Grammar, South Killingly, and East Killingly schools were then closed. The last of the old schools in Attawaugan, Ballouville, and Dayville were closed when the new Killingly Central School opened in 1959. H. H. Ellis Technical School was built in 1958, the new Killingly High School in 1965, followed by a state regional community college in 1971. Killingly Intermediate School in Dayville was dedicated in 1990 and Quinebaug Valley Community College completed a major addition in 2006.

Aspinwall Cemetery, the oldest cemetery in the original town boundaries, is located on Route 12 in Putnam. Breakneck Burying Ground was established about 1743. It is believed the first person buried there was Capt. Ephraim Warren in 1747. There are 70 cemeteries located within the present boundaries of Killingly.

FIRST CHURCH OF KILLINGLY. The original township of Killingly, begun about 1700, originally included the present towns of Thompson, Killingly and most of Putnam. The region now known as Putnam Heights was called Killingly Hill. The church was organized October 15, 1715, and held services in an early frame structure. The church building there now is the third meetinghouse to be built in the vicinity and was completed around December 1818.

TEMPLE BETH ISRAEL, KILLINGLY DRIVE. From the formation in 1949 of the Danielson Jewish Community Club with meetings held in a member's home, grew the idea that a synagogue could be built to be a center for the local Jewish families. Designed in 1951 by architect William Riseman of Boston, the basic building was completed by the end of 1953.

OLD METHODIST CHURCH. Major repairs were started on the church in Danielson on the corner of Main and Central Streets in August 1867. The church was raised from the sills four feet, and a new front and a steeple were added. New circular windows were put in, as well as a new pulpit and a new singing gallery. The cost was about $6,000. The architect for the work was Alexander G. Cutler of Norwich. N. C. Bowen was in charge of the improvements and E. N. Eldridge did the painting. P. T. Butler of Boston did the frescos, and Franklin Clark made the pulpit. In March 1874, a beautiful chandelier with 12 burners was hung in the church. (Courtesy of the Killingly Public Library Archives.)

INTERIOR OF OLD METHODIST CHURCH. A bell was ordered from Troy, New York. It weighed 1,049 pounds and was placed in the 120-foot spire. Unfortunately the bell did not arrive in time for the dedication in January 1868, but made its appearance the Saturday after. In January 1880, it was announced that they feared the bell in the church spire was cracked. A brick-walled basement called Washington Hall was built beneath the church. In later years, the members finally felt this busy corner was too noisy, so a new church was built on Spring Street in 1902. (Courtesy of the Killingly Public Library Archives.)

ATTAWAUGAN SCHOOL. The school in District No. 8 was built sometime between 1870 and 1880. It was a wooden structure of two stories located on Country Club Road, just off Route 12. There were four rooms used to house eight grades. Outhouse facilities were used up until the late 1940s. At the time of closing in 1957, there were six grades being taught with the upper two grades being bussed to Danielson.

BALLOUVILLE SCHOOL. The school was identified on the 1869 town map as District No. 9. In 1876, the school visitors (officials who rated the schools and teachers) recommended a new schoolhouse be built to better accommodate the students. It closed in the early 1950s. Since 1963, the LaBelle-Lemieux American Legion Post No. 183 has owned it.

NEW ST. JAMES SCHOOL, DANIELSON. The new St. James School on Water Street was dedicated January 8, 1956, under the directorship of the Reverend Bernard J. Flanagan, D.D., First Bishop of Norwich, during the pastorate of the Reverend Leo J. Martel. Over 1,000 people attended the ceremony.

ST. JAMES CLASS OF 1938. It should be fun to see how many people can be identified in this photograph. Two that are known are Gabriel Barrette and Joseph Bertorelli. The Killingly Historical Society appreciates help in identifying old photographs. (Courtesy of Patricia Bertorelli Belade.)

84

KILLINGLY MEMORIAL SCHOOL, DANIELSON. The new school at the corner of Main and Hutchins Streets was dedicated at a ceremony on May 3, 1953, beginning with a parade through town and a flag raising. On November 13, 1995, a plaque honoring veterans of World War II who raised money for the school's construction was dedicated. The veterans raised $25,000, and Crystal Water Company matched it to be used for a community room where veterans could hold their meetings.

GRACE STANTON'S FIRST CLASS, 1909. Grace Stanton was a brand new teacher as she stepped in front of the sixth grade class in the Danielson Grammar School on High Street. She continued teaching that grade until her retirement in 1944. The classroom was on the second floor of the school. Note the inkwells on the right side of each desk. Some boys were known to try to dunk the girl's pigtails in them.

KILLINGLY HIGH SCHOOL, 1890. This is one of the classes in what was known later as the Danielson Grammar School. The high school classes were under the management of Professor A. P. Somes, and the school was ranked among the best in the state. A classroom was built under the bell tower to house the commercial department of the high school. (Courtesy of Thomas Guillemette.)

NEW KILLINGLY HIGH SCHOOL, DANIELSON. The new Killingly High School opened on Westfield Avenue in September 1965. It was built around a center courtyard. After its opening, the town's school programs were revised. Grades 1–6 were at the three elementary schools, grades 7–8 were at the junior high (former high school), and grades 9–12 were at the new high school building.

GOODYEAR SCHOOL, ROGERS. A new school was built on Williamsville Road in Goodyear and dedicated June 6, 1948, replacing the one that burned in May 1945. It housed grades 1 through 8 until 1952, grades 1 through 6 from 1952 to 1967, and 1 through 4 until 1968. In 1969, the school system was revamped, and Goodyear School became the kindergarten for the entire town of Killingly, opening with 221 pupils. It is now the Goodyear Early Learning Center. (Courtesy of the Town of Killingly files.)

KILLINGLY HIGH SCHOOL, 1898. Seen here are, from left to right, (first row) two unidentified, Dyer Potter, unidentified, Helen L. Tillinghast (Pellett), and unidentified; (second row) two unidentified, Cora Logee, and Josephine Danielson (Walker); (third row) unidentified, Marion D. Chollar (teacher), unidentified, Abby Nutter, and Alice Sweet (Lamb); (fourth row) four unidentified, A. P. Somes (principal), and unidentified. (Courtesy of Henry Hopkins.)

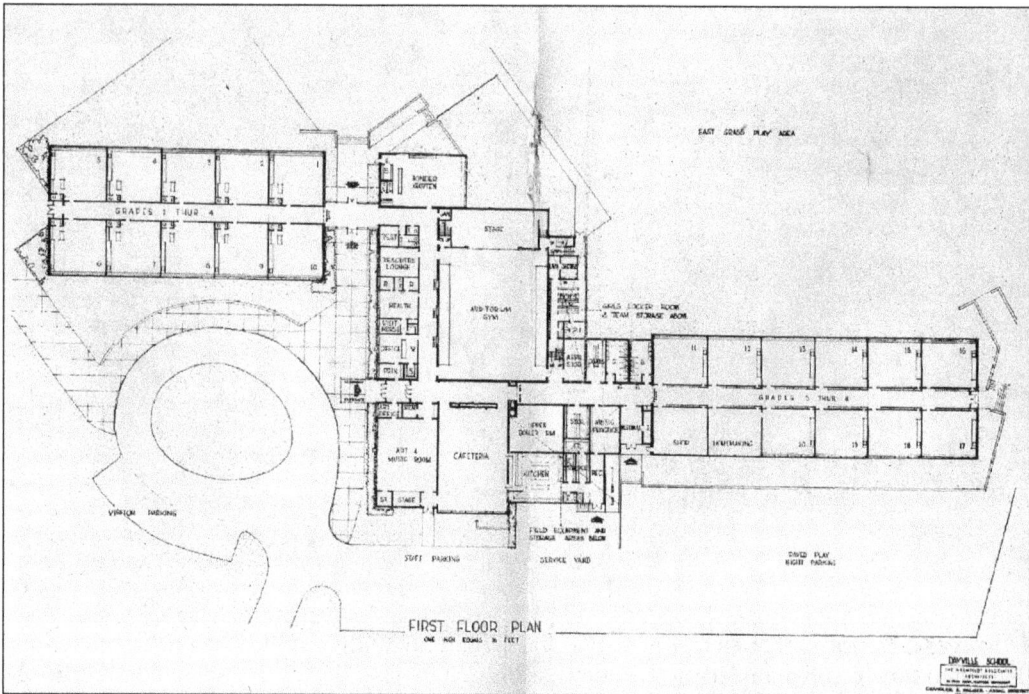

KILLINGLY CENTRAL SCHOOL. Funds were appropriated in October 1956 for a new school in Dayville on Soap Street to be placed on a portion of the town farm property. It opened September 1958, with 626 students enrolled and began a new era in elementary education. All students were housed in three schools: Goodyear, Killingly Memorial School, and Killingly Central School. (Courtesy of the Town of Killingly files.)

KILLINGLY INTERMEDIATE SCHOOL, DAYVILLE. As a culmination of five years of planning and investigation, the dedication of Killingly's new intermediate school took place September 9, 1990. The doors of the school on Upper Maple Street opened with over 870 students and 80 staff members. The fifth and sixth grades are segregated from the seventh and eighth grades in separate wings, each grade occupying a single floor. (Courtesy of the Town of Killingly files.)

HARVARD H. ELLIS TECHNICAL VOCATIONAL SCHOOL, DANIELSON. In June 1956, the Killingly Alumni Association transferred the land they had originally purchased from James Danielson to the State of Connecticut. The Alumni Field on Maple Street was selected as the site for a new regional trade school. It was to be known as the Harvard H. Ellis Technical Vocational School in tribute to Harvard Ellis, the former director of the Putnam Technical School. The school was dedicated November 8, 1959.

QUINEBAUG VALLEY COMMUNITY COLLEGE, DANIELSON. Quinebaug Valley Community College opened September 27, 1971, with 215 students and eight full-time professional employees. Construction of the college campus in the current location on Upper Maple Street was dedicated June 1983. The West Wing opened in October 2006 to provide the current 1,750 credit students, non-credit students, and the community with additional classroom spaces, an art gallery, and faculty offices. (Courtesy of Quinebaug Valley Community College.)

ASPINWALL CEMETERY. Aspinwall Cemetery on Route 12 is the oldest cemetery within the original town boundaries but is now located in Putnam. Many of Killingly's early settlers are buried here dating back to the mid-1700s including Rev. Aaron Brown and Rev. Perley Howe, ministers of the First Church of Killingly; John Felshaw; Nell Alexander, son of the first Nell Alexander; Joseph Cady; and Joseph Leavens.

PUTNAM HEIGHTS CEMETERY. Another old cemetery that once was part of Killingly is on Route 21 on Putnam Heights. It is the final resting place of more of the town's early settlers, including a son of William Rhodes Rawson, the furniture maker; Rev. Elisha Atkins, minister of the First Church of Killingly; Dr. Robert Grosvenor; Dr. Edward Mowrey Harris; Col. Hobart Torrey; and Fenner Harris Peckham.

HOLY CROSS CEMETERY, MAPLE STREET, DANIELSON. The new St. James Cemetery was consecrated on October 27, 1910, with 300–400 members of the parish gathered for the event. There is a great cross that rises from a circular mound in the center of the burying ground. It is now known as Holy Cross Cemetery.

OLD WESTFIELD CEMETERY, NORTH STREET, DANIELSON. According to the *History of Windham County, Connecticut*, in his declining years, James Danielson "laid out a burial ground between the rivers for the use of the inhabitants and was the first to be interred in it." He died January 22, 1728, at the age of 80. Stones bearing the names of many early Killingly families are found in this old cemetery. The new cemetery is located across the street.

CROSS ROADS CEMETERY, DAYVILLE. This cemetery has also been called the "Day Yard" or the "Old Killingly Yard." It is located at Dayville Four Corners (the junction of Routes 12 and 101). The earliest burials date back to 1792 for members of the Day family. Other names that are familiar in Killingly history include Prosper Alexander and Barzillia Fisher.

HIGH STREET CEMETERY, DAYVILLE. This cemetery is the burial place of Col. William Alexander (1787–1875) and many others in the Alexander family. It is also the final resting place of many other significant families, including the Cogswells, Blanchards, Days, Jencks, Sayles, and Russells.

Four

PEOPLE AT
WORK AND PLAY

As in all communities, the people of Killingly divided their time between work and play. In the early days of the settlement, most of the day was spent working. Arduous tasks that machines perform today were only accomplished by backbreaking labor. Sawmills were required to provide lumber for homes and other buildings. Farming required the use of horses and oxen until the advent of the combustion engine. Large groups of men did the work of building local roads, even shoveling the snow from those roads in the winter.

Recreation and entertainment evolved over the years from church-related functions to many different sports, fraternal organizations, and literary entertainments. As free time increased, so did the variety of activities available to try such as velocipede riding in 1874, roller skating and ice skating, inside walking matches in 1879, and glass ball and target shooting in 1883. Modern times now provide a wide variety of entertainment via radio, television, the Internet, and travel. People have more time to devote to play than ever before.

Killingly is the birthplace of many notable people. Charles Lewis Tiffany, founder of Tiffany and Company in New York City was born in Killingly. The early Alexander family produced a well-known artist, Francis Alexander. William Torrey Harris, a widely known public school educator in the United States in the 19th century, was named fourth commissioner of education by Pres. Benjamin Harrison in 1835 and served for 17 years. Again in the 20th century, a Killingly native, Dr. Sidney P. Marland Jr., was selected by Pres. Richard Nixon for commissioner of education. U.S. District Court judge T. Emmet Clarie grew up in Goodyear (now Rogers). National League baseball umpire Frank Dascoli was a popular athlete at Killingly High School. Betty Tianti was the nation's first woman president of a state AFL-CIO federation. Several athletes have gone on to play in the major leagues in football, baseball, and basketball as well as boxing, namely Eric Laakso (Miami Dolphins), Roger LeFrancois (Red Sox), Tracy Lis (Blizzards in the American Basketball League), and Lou Brouillard (inducted into the International Boxing Hall of Fame in 2006). Killingly had its share of inventors, too. Those of note were Mary Dixon Kies and Charles H. Bacon.

KILLINGLY BOARD OF SELECTMEN, 1915. Killingly's earlier form of government that led the town was the board of selectmen. Seen here in 1915, from left to right, these men are H. Place, Louis Young, John Gilbert, Frank Whipple, and A. P. Burns. Wesley Wilson, bookkeeper, is standing. (Courtesy of Richard Ouellette.)

KILLINGLY TOWN COUNCIL, 1993. A new Killingly Charter was adopted in 1969 providing a town manager–town council form of government. The first nine-member town council was sworn in November 1970. Seen here are council members for 1993. They are, from left to right, (first row) David LaBelle, James Vance, Linda Wojcik, town manager Thomas Homan, and Joyce Eber; (second row) Joseph Bove, Philip Hoyt, Stewart Rivers, David Griffiths, Jack Burke, and Terry Sandsbury. (Courtesy of the Town of Killingly files.)

MANUAL LABOR. These three trucks in the photograph probably date somewhere between 1926 and 1930. However, since there are 28 men with shovels ready to fill them with gravel, this photograph may have been from the WPA era of the 1930s, when so many men were out of work and were given jobs on various government projects. (Courtesy of Patricia Bertorelli Belade.)

KILLINGLY DEPARTMENT OF PUBLIC WORKS. In 1890, the town tried out a six-horse road-scraper that could repair more road than a dozen men. Then times changed and work on town projects became more mechanized. Members of the Killingly Department of Public Works crew are shown resurfacing part of the town's 130 miles of roads. The Town Garage is on the old Town Farm property on Route 12 in Dayville. (Courtesy of the Town of Killingly files.)

OLD MAN WITH FIDDLE AND TELESCOPE. William Prescott Aldrich came from the Sparks district of East Killingly. His was a life of unusual adventures. He spent four years on a whaling voyage going through ice floes in the Arctic, deserting ship in Australia, and visiting primitive barbarians in Japan. He returned in 1857 and became a brick and stone layer. He loved astronomy and fitted up an observatory with a high-powered telescope. (Courtesy of Henry Hopkins.)

BOROUGH POLICE FORCE. Shown in this photograph are, from left to right, Richard Levola, John Blanchette, Gerald Bissonnette, Mary O'Connell, borough president Ellis Howland, Chief Albert Rivers, Sgt. William Hartley, Leopold Poirier, Nicholas Peters, Normand Dumont, William Vargas, and Henry Lefevre. They are standing in front of the police annex of the Danielson Fire Station.

DAYVILLE CAR BARN YARD. The car barn for the trolleys was on the northeast corner of Lake Road and Route 101. Shown is the Providence and Danielson Express Car No. 1274. This was a busy place in the early 1900s. (Courtesy of Henry Hopkins.)

TROLLEY CONDUCTOR AND MOTORMAN. Clarence L. Chandler Sr., conductor, and Walter E. Card, motorman, pause from their duties at the Dayville Car Barn in 1910. These trolley cars ran from Webster Center in Massachusetts to Central Village, Connecticut, a distance of almost 28 miles. They had been working on the cars since 1901.

MILITIA TRAINING GROUNDS, ROUTE 21, PUTNAM HEIGHTS. The broad common area on Killingly Hill north of the First Church of Killingly was used as the training grounds for the militiamen and for military parades. In 1775, the Connecticut General Assembly ordered the entire militia to muster and drill once a week for the next three months. Six companies marched from Killingly to answer the Lexington Alarm, led by Maj. William Danielson.

SPANISH AMERICAN WAR UNIT. Michael McShane of East Killingly is the soldier on the extreme right with a bugle. He is buried in the Bartlett Cemetery in East Killingly. There were men from Killingly who served their country in every war. (Courtesy of Henry Hopkins.)

GALLUP'S POND, STEARNS HILL FARM, DANIELSON. Every winter from 1925 to 1945, John Gallup of Stearns Hill Farm blocked a drainage culvert with sandbags so the water protected the cranberry bushes growing there. The deepest spot anywhere was only about three feet. All winter folks skated there. Near the end of each season, Gallup asked some of the young local boys to sprinkle sand on the ice as cranberries thrive in a sandy soil. In the 1940s and early 1950s the Stearns Hill Dairy was situated in front of the pond beside the house. It was a favorite spot for hot dogs and hamburgers as well a cone of delicious ice cream. It was run by Gene Mercier, whose day job was industrial arts teacher at Killingly High School. (Above, courtesy of Barbara Bourque; below, courtesy of the Killingly Public Library Archives.)

DAUGHTERS OF ISABELLA NO. 633. The group of women was organized on February 4, 1940, and meetings were held at the town hall. The name, Star of the Sea, was chosen for the circle. Bertha Carragher was the first regent. This is a photograph of the first anniversary celebration in 1941, held in the Polish American Clubhouse on Water Street in Danielson. (Courtesy of Patricia Bertorelli Belade.)

ACME COTTON COMPANY BAND, EAST KILLINGLY. Starting about 1867, bands and orchestras were organized in nearly every village. Men acquired instruments and diligently learned to play them. They hired professionals to instruct and conduct them. They raised money for uniforms and soon were playing frequent concerts to entertain the townspeople. Included in this group were Vernon West, Raymond Withey, Claude Moran, and Carlton Smith. (Courtesy of Henry Hopkins.)

DR. WILLIAM TORREY HARRIS. Dr. William Harris was born in North Killingly, now Putnam, on September 10, 1835. He was a well-known educator and philosopher during the 19th century. He served as U.S. commissioner of education from 1889 to 1906 under Presidents Grover Cleveland, William McKinley, and Theodore Roosevelt. His wife, Sarah (Bugbee) Harris, was niece of Edwin Holmes Bugbee, for whom the Killingly Historical Center building was named. He died on November 5, 1909.

DR. SIDNEY P. MARLAND JR. Sidney P. Marland Jr. was born in Danielson on August 19, 1914. During World War II, he served in the U.S. Army in the Pacific and Washington, D.C., directing Pacific military intelligence research for the U.S. Department of War. Marland was nominated by Pres. Richard Nixon as the U.S. commissioner of education, taking office December 17, 1970, for a period of 3.5 years. He died May 25, 1992. (Courtesy of the Sidney P. Marland Jr. Collection, Killingly Historical and Genealogical Society.)

C. H. BACON INVENTION. C. H. Bacon held patents for three of his inventions which he had produced and sold or used in his business. One was for the wallpaper exhibitor patented August 20, 1889, which he is demonstrating here; it could hold 200 samples of paper with border attached. He also had other patents. The original patents are now the property of the Killingly Historical Society.

MARY DIXON KIES. Mary Dixon Kies of South Killingly received the first known patent issued to a woman in the United States for her "new and useful improvement in weaving straw with silk or thread" on May 5, 1809, signed by Pres. James A. Madison. A memorial stone for her is beside that of her husband, John Kies, in the old South Killingly Cemetery. She died in 1837. (Courtesy of the Killingly Public Library Archives.)

CORN CUTTER (PATENT 1876). Following in the footsteps of his grandfather Benjamin Jacobs, who was a plow maker, William O. Jacobs patented and sold agricultural tools as well as running a large and well-appointed hardware store. The corn cutter was used by farmers to chop the feed for their animals. It is on display in the Killingly Historical Society's museum. (Courtesy of George Meehan.)

DANIELSON BUSINESSMEN, C. 1924. In 1924, Louis Bertorelli, left, and Joseph Cristina, right, became partners in the New York Fruit Store on Main Street in Danielson. Bertorelli took over as sole owner in 1928. Cristina later became manager of the Attawaugan Hotel in Danielson. The store stayed in the Bertorelli family for many years. Later it was purchased by Aldo and Wanda Cassetari. (Courtesy of Patricia Bertorelli Belade.)

DANIELSON ATHLETIC CLUB, 1939–1940. The girls' basketball team played preliminary games for the Danielson men's basketball team. The members of the girls' team, seen here from left to right, are (first row) Dot Hutchins, Jeannette LaBelle, and Simone Bouthillier; (second row) Wanda Slowick; (third row) Dot Friese, Julie Macina, Wanda Grondelski, Bea Myers, Kay Carragher, Simone Rounds, and Dot Barrows. Their coach was Frank Dascoli. (Courtesy of Dorothy Hutchins Pryor.)

ERIK LAAKSO. The Miami Dolphins drafted football player Erik Laakso in 1978 in round four to play offensive guard and offensive tackle. During the next seven years, he played in 86 games. He was born November 29, 1956, and graduated from Killingly High School and Tulane University. (Courtesy of the Miami Dolphins.)

OLD FURNACE STATE PARK
KILLINGLY, CONN.

OLD FURNACE STATE PARK. A beautiful area on Horse Hill Road in South Killingly was made a state park in 1944. In those early years, the Red Cross gave swimming lessons to hundreds of young children each summer in this pool. In 1835, an iron foundry was located there, thus the reason for its name. Earlier yet, there had been a gristmill and later a plaster mill. (Courtesy of Joseph Chauvin.)

MADDEN'S GROVE. In 1865, this delightful place was known as Madden's Grove, near Dayville, owned by Frank Madden. The lake was called Saunders' Pond in the early days. It had swings and tables, boats for sailing parties, was equipped for clambakes, and had a hall for dancing. It is now called Alexander's Lake. (Courtesy of Thomas Guillemette.)

FISTICUFFS WITH THE GUYS. Claude Moran and James Aldrich of East Killingly do not seem to be too serious about this little altercation. The fellow in the rear is unidentified. (Courtesy of Henry Hopkins.)

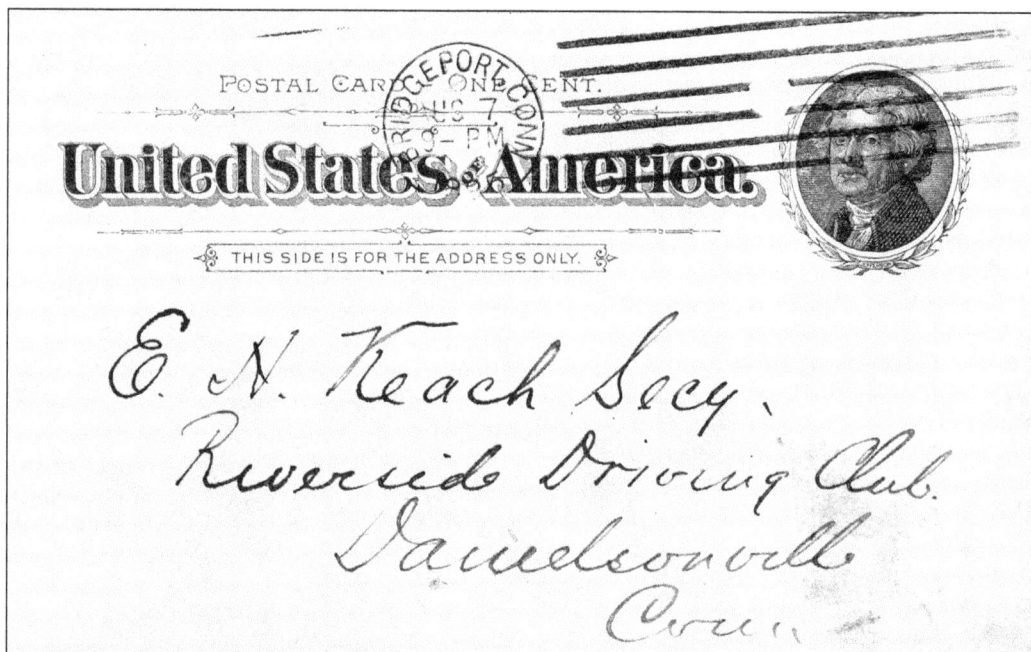

POSTAL CARD ONE CENT.

United States of America.

THIS SIDE IS FOR THE ADDRESS ONLY.

E. N. Keach Secy.
Riverside Driving Club.
Danielsonville
Conn.

KILLINGLY'S RIVERSIDE DRIVING CLUB. In the spring of 1894, the Riverside Driving Club was building a half-mile trotting track off Maple Street in Danielson. A high board enclosure surrounded the club's property. There were barns, sheds, and a grandstand. The street bordering the grounds was widened to allow three teams to go abreast. There was another trotting park built near Alexander's Lake in 1870 by Leander Sayles. (Courtesy of Thomas Guillemette.)

CHARLES L. TIFFANY (1812–1902). Charles L. Tiffany was born in Killingly on February 15, 1812. Pictured here is his later home on South Main Street in East Brooklyn. Tiffany kept a factory store near the mill for his father, Comfort Tiffany. In 1853, Charles and Eben Young went to New York City, where they started a jewelry firm under the name of Tiffany and Young, which eventually became the celebrated Charles L. Tiffany Company. (Courtesy of the Killingly Public Library Archives.)

JUDGE T. EMMET CLARIE'S HOME. The c. 1800 colonial home on Peckham Lane in Danielson was once owned by William K. Pike, who was a prominent local surveyor. It was later purchased by T. Emmet Clarie, a local attorney. He was appointed to the federal bench by Pres. John F. Kennedy in 1961. Clarie was perhaps best known for the Hartford trial of the 16 defendants accused of stealing $7 million from Wells Fargo. (Courtesy of the Killingly Public Library Archives.)

EBENEZER YOUNG HOUSE, C. 1845. This house on North Main Street in Danielson once belonged to Killingly leading citizen, attorney, judge, politician, and mill owner Ebenezer Young. Originally smaller, the building was a private academic school owned by Stowell L. Weld and was sold to Young in the mid-1840s. In the 1920s and 1930s, it was occupied by Young's three spinster daughters. (Courtesy of the Killingly Public Library Archives.)

CAPRON HOUSE, C. 1880–1883. The earliest owner of this house on Main Street in Danielson was lawyer Thomas Backus, who sold it to wealthy cotton waste dealer Orville M. Capron in 1855. It was modified from an earlier, smaller house. Later owners were the Bacon family and attorney Basil T. Tsakonas.

Five

OLD MEMORIES

The past 300 years have seen great changes in the modes of transportation in Killingly. The earliest, of course, were the horse and buggy or wagon, as well as the hard-working oxen. Besides taking people from place to place, they were essential in tilling the soil, hauling logs or heavy loads, and in harvesting the grains and hay. These animals served in this capacity for the first 200 years of the town's life.

Stagecoaches provided the link between the town's villages and other towns and cities. In addition to carrying passengers, their most important task was bringing the mail. Taverns and inns were conveniently located along the routes to provide food and shelter for travelers and a change of horses.

The advent of the railroad in 1840 brought changes to Dayville and Danielsonville. The centers of population and business shifted from the clusters around the mills and near the rivers and streams to be closer to the railroad depots in the two villages in particular. New streets had to be laid out to accommodate businesses and homes that changed the character of the villages.

Railroad transportation was joined early in the 1900s by the electric railroad (trolleys), buses, and the automobile. Businesses, as well as private homes, were electrified and telephones were installed from 1882 to 1889. For a time, the streets of the town held a mixture of horses and buggies and the newfangled cars. The town now boasts an airport that continues to be modernized. A network of highways and turnpikes has been improved and provides the town's residents with connections to the major cities of the northeast and the rest of the country.

Reading about the history of the town and looking at the photographs spark old memories of days gone by, people some have known, and places some have seen. Without the photographs, many of those sights might be forgotten.

DAVIS PARK FOUNTAIN. Exciting news was shared in May 1890 when the announcement was made that Honorable Almond M. Paine, a prominent citizen of the town and judge of probate for several years, told Davis Park trustees that he would place a handsome fountain in the new park. They anticipated the cost to be about $500 and said it would be placed on the highest spot of the park, near its center. (Courtesy of the McEwen Collection, Killingly Historical and Genealogical Society.)

BANDSTAND, DAVIS PARK, DANIELSON. The deed to about two acres of land in Danielsonville known as the Cutler lot was given to trustees of the park association in September 1889 by Edwin Davis as a memorial for his parents, Randall and Phillia Kies Davis. Money to purchase the bandstand was raised by ladies of the town to be placed not far from the fountain. (Courtesy of Thomas Guillemette.)

HORSE DRINKING FOUNTAINS. In 1890, a fund was started to raise money to buy and install two water fountains for horses, believing in humanity for beasts as well as men. They were ordered in July 1891. One ornamental fountain was placed at the corner of Reynolds and Main Streets. As the second picture shows, it was used in winter too, as horses passed by pulling their sleighs. The second fountain is shown in the photograph on the next page. (Above, courtesy of the Killingly Public Library Archives; below, courtesy of the Alice M. Bacon Collection, Killingly Historical and Genealogical Society.)

PARADE CROSSING FRANKLIN STREET BRIDGE. A Danielsonville parade on lower Franklin Street marched across the stone arch bridge that was built in 1889. It was built by stonemason Thomas Bradford at a cost of $5,000. It is not known exactly when the parade took place, but it would have been some time after 1890. The other horse fountain was situated near the twin bridges at the foot of Main Street and the end of Franklin Street as shown in the above photograph. The bridge was removed in 1957 to make way for the rotary at the lower end of Main Street. (Courtesy of Richard Ouellette.)

DANIELSON PARADE, C. 1945. Parades have been a way of celebrating for centuries. This group is marching past the Attawaugan Hotel that housed the F. W. Woolworth Company on the ground floor. On the left was Lord's Shoe Store. On the right is the Astoria Restaurant that was in the Evergates Building. This may have been in 1945 at the end of World War II. (Courtesy of Patricia Bertorelli Belade.)

THE FROGS
OF
WINDHAM

TO BE GIVEN IN

Music Hall, Danielson,
THURSDAY AND FRIDAY EVENINGS,
APRIL 27 AND 28, 1905,

UNDER THE AUSPICES OF

MECHANICS BAND

75═══People in the Cast═══75

Splendid Spectacular Scenes,
Gorgeous Costumes, - - Beautiful Music.

Peep! Cachug! Better-go-round and see the
Frisky, Frolicsome Frogs.

RESERVED SEATS, 35 and 50 Cents.
On Sale at Barron's Music Store.

MUSIC HALL PROGRAM, 1905. The people of Danielson were proud of their fine Music Hall and the varied programs that were held there. *The Frogs of Windham* was an operetta telling the story of an historic event in Windham County. (Courtesy of Richard Ouellette.)

OLD RED HOUSE, BROAD STREET, C. 1781. Probably the oldest house in Danielson, it was purchased by Stephen Rickard in 1838, and his daughter stated it was then thought to be 81 years old, but further research figures the building date was closer to 1781. It was probably built by Zadock Spalding who, with his wife, Hannah, were charter members of the Westfield Congregational Church. Zadock Spalding was born in Killingly on May 8, 1746.

J. ALDEN DANIELSON HOUSE. This historic house on Upper Maple Street was built in three different periods, the earliest around 1750 and the latest about 1880. The land has been, and still is, in the Danielson family since 1707 when James Danielson came here from Block Island, Rhode Island. Part of this land is where the Quinebaug Community College now stands. (Courtesy of the Killingly Public Library Archives.)

114

STREET SPRINKLER. William Gleason, with his original but effective sprinkling machine, appeared in the streets in May 1872. Local businessmen felt sure that the cart would not stop for want of funds. There were very few things they contributed for with more pleasure than the watering cart, especially in dry and dusty times. Gleason did this for a number of years. (Courtesy of Joseph Chauvin.)

MAIN STREET IN THE LOWER VILLAGE, C. 1900. The men are heading home from work at the Williamsville Manufacturing Company in Williamsville (later named Goodyear and then renamed Rogers). That part of the village was the victim of nature's forces during the 1936 flood, the 1938 hurricane, and another flood in 1955. (Courtesy of the McEwen Collection)

BURGESS HAY FIELD, DANIELSON. At one time the major portion of the area east of Broad Street in Danielson was farmland. Pictured is one of Ezra Burgess's hay fields between Route 6 and Reynolds Street. The tree in the left foreground is approximately where Haven Health Care is now located. (Courtesy of Barbara Bourque.)

EZRA BURGESS AND FRIEND. The old farmers generally had some animal they were especially proud of. For some it was a pair of oxen or a beautiful horse; but for Ezra Burgess of Reynolds Street, it was his prize bull. The large tub in the carriage shed was used when it was time to slaughter the pigs. (Courtesy of Barbara Bourque.)

116

NORTH MAIN STREET, ELMVILLE. The area on the left side of North Main Street is where the drive-in theater was once located. Note the tracks on the right side of the road for the trolley. Poles were on both sides of the road; evidently those on the right carried the power for the trolley and those on the left were for telephone lines. (Courtesy of the McEwen Collection)

LOWER MAIN STREET, DANIELSON. The two houses on the left were the last houses on the Danielson side before the bridge to Brooklyn. They were razed when the traffic circle was reconfigured in 1957. The photograph caught the era marking the change from horse and carriage to automobile. (Courtesy of the McEwen Collection, Killingly Historical and Genealogical Society.)

BROAD STREET SCENE. A letter to the editor was sent to the *Windham County Transcript* in 1890 complaining of "Racing on the Boulevard." Many fast horses from different localities were among the racers and a great many spectators were present, although it was against the law to race horses or coast on a public thoroughfare. The complaint was that the authorities forbade coasting but allowed horse racing. (Courtesy of the McEwen Collection, Killingly Historical and Genealogical Society.)

MAIN STREET, DANIELSON, C. 1900. This photograph illustrates two of the modes of transportation that were available at that time. A horse and buggy wait patiently for the owner on the left. In the center is the electric railway (trolley). Main Street is bustling with shoppers. The building on the right of the town hall is the Dexter Building, built in 1882 by Edward Dexter at a cost of about $20,000.

MAIN STREET, DANIELSON. A more modern era is shown on this post card. At that time the Rexall Drug Store was on the corner of Main and Central Streets with the Smart Shoppe next door and People's Loan Company on the second floor. The next store is in the old Methodist Parsonage, then Dowe's, the LaClair and Savings Bank buildings, and Bargain Supply Company on the corner of Main and Academy Streets. (Courtesy of Joseph Chauvin.)

RAILROAD CROSSING, DANIELSON, C. 1957. On the right is Dragon's Barber Shop, owned by Esidore Dragon. The Danielson Inn, also facing Furnace Street, was owned by John and Josephine Polanski. The stone building in the middle was the office of Anthony and Alfred Stedman's Danielson Taxi, torn down in 1974. The Dayville Grain and Feed Company is behind the railroad gate tender's shack. On the far left is the back of Duffy's Diner.

BALLOUVILLE STREET SCENE. This early photograph shows a scene of a quiet rural road in the village of Ballouville. A combination of small farms and mill tenement houses were in the area that made up the villages of Ballouville and Pineville near the mills. (Courtesy of Thomas Guillemette.)

BALLOUVILLE BUS. The Ballouville Store in the background is also the village's post office. It was constructed around 1845 by mill owners Jabez Amsbury and Leonard Ballou, and it has housed the post office since 1882. It is considered the best preserved of the mid-19th century mill village stores in Killingly. (Courtesy of Margaret Weaver.)

120

BOYS AVENUE, GOODYEAR. In 1919, the Goodyear Company constructed an entirely new village called Goodyear Heights for their expanding workforce. Boys Avenue was named for Robert Boys who was the mill agent. It was accepted as an official town street on October 7, 1935. Through his efforts, the ethnic character of the village was diversified, as he recruited Polish and Portuguese workers. (Courtesy of Thomas Guillemette.)

SOUTH KILLINGLY STONE ARCH BRIDGE. The small stone arch bridge on Cook Hill Road between the two cemeteries is a small example of bridge building that has been handed down from the early Romans. Very few materials have greater compressive strength than cut stone, so the bridges can handle heavy loads safely. Killingly still has some of these bridges in use.

LONGO LADIES. Here three of the ladies who lived on Water Street in Danielson can be seen. The photograph was probably taken in the late 1920s. They are, from left to right, Carolina Longo, Lorena Longo, and Nellie Longo. The factory in the background is the Danielson Worsted Company. (Courtesy of Patricia Bertorelli Belade.)

WESTFIELD ACADEMY. A private school was built on Broad Street at the head of Academy Street in 1847 in order to fill Killingly's need for its own secondary school. Previously students had to travel to Plainfield or Woodstock to complete high school. The school was closed in 1852. The property was purchased by St. Alban's Episcopal Church, who later built a church there. (Courtesy of Thomas Guillemette.)

DANIELSON SPRINGTIME FESTIVAL, 2005. The Danielson Springtime Festival began in 1971 as the brainchild of Killingly High School band director Jerre Fillmore. It was meant to lift the spirits of Killingly's residents. With support of the town's young businessmen, Fillmore and Louis A. Woisard Jr. began planning. It progressed from a three-day affair in 1971 to a two-week event by the late 1980s. Crowds of folks turn out for this gala festival. (Courtesy of Charleen's Portrait Studio.)

CELEBRATION PARADE. According to *Miles of Millstreams,* by Weaver, Wood, and Wood, "the Bicentennial celebrations for the town of Killingly highlighted the summer of 1908. Under the chairmanship of Timothy Hopkins, elaborate programs were planned for July 2–5. Opening ceremonies on Thursday featured the dedication and open house at the new high school on Broad Street." (Courtesy of the McEwen Collection, Killingly Historical and Genealogical Society.)

BICENTENNIAL SIGN. Friday, July 3, 1908, was designated Governor's Day during the bicentennial celebrations. Activities commenced with a baseball game on the Quinebaug Company grounds in Danielson; the Wauregan Grays of the Eastern Connecticut League played the C.A.C. of Norwich. Following the game, Gov. Rollin S. Woodruff was greeted with a 17-gun salute. (Courtesy of the McEwen Collection, Killingly Historical and Genealogical Society.)

PARADE HORSES AND WAGONS. The grand parade of military, firemen, civic societies, floats, and automobiles followed the baseball game. Speakers during the afternoon exercises at Davis Park were Governor Woodruff; Senator Frank B. Brandegee; Samuel D. Hart, D.D.; Emma C. Hammond; Ellen D. Larned; and Honorable Edgar M. Warner. Music was provided by the Mechanics Band. (Courtesy of the McEwen Collection, Killingly Historical and Genealogical Society.)

PARADE ROUTE. Saturday at 4:00 a.m., there was the "National salute of 46 guns, ringing of bells, blowing of whistles, and general awakening," according to *Miles of Millstreams*. The Parade of Antiques and Horribles commenced at 7:00 a.m.; masks for participants were provided free of charge at Dowe's Book Store. Music was provided by Professor Shoebuckles' Band and Day's Drum Corps. A 46-gun national salute occurred again at noon. (Courtesy of the McEwen Collection, Killingly Historical and Genealogical Society.)

MAIN STREET PARADE ROUTE. On Friday evening, Davis Park was the site of a band concert by the St. James Band and a grand fireworks display. On the afternoon and evening of Saturday, the Fourth of July, activities included band concerts by the Mechanics Band and St. James Band, baseball at Wildwood Park (Dayville versus Wauregan), and vaudeville at Wildwood Park. (Courtesy of the McEwen Collection, Killingly Historical and Genealogical Society.)

REFRESHMENT STAND. Looking closely at the picture, boys and girls can be seen clustered around a keg perched on a stand on the corner of Main and Academy Streets in Danielson. Since there was no one around to collect money, it probably held water for thirsty parade watchers. Photographs taken throughout the parade show that this was a popular stop for young and old alike. (Courtesy of the McEwen Collection, Killingly Historical and Genealogical Society.)

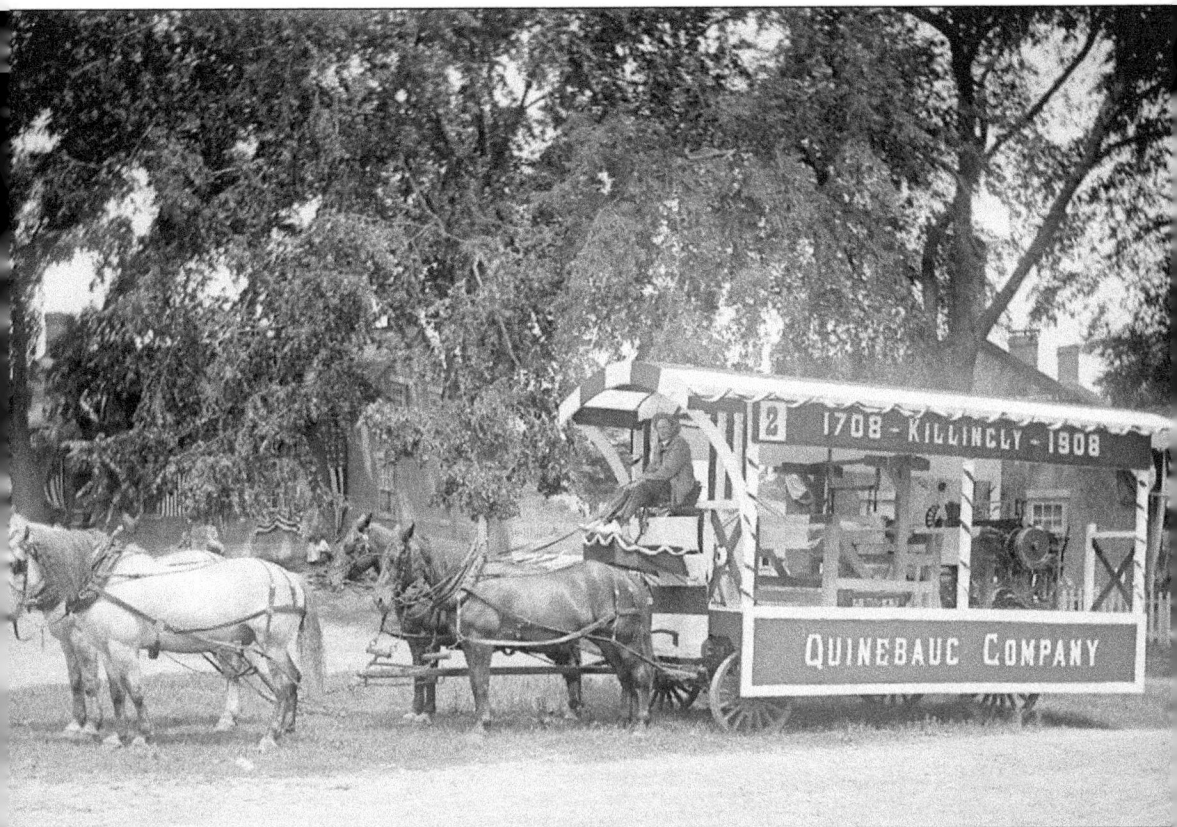

BICENTENNIAL PARADE FLOAT. Many companies provided decorated floats for the parade. The Quinebaug Company even had textile machinery exhibited on their float. The end of the celebration was held in area churches at their morning services. Closing exercises took place in the historic Westfield Church. (Courtesy of the McEwen Collection, Killingly Historical and Genealogical Society.)

Visit us at
arcadiapublishing.com